Painted
Birdhouses

Painted
Birdhouses

Sterling Publishing Co., Inc. New York
A Sterling / Chapelle Book

Chapelle, Ltd.:

- Owner: Jo Packham
- Editor: Laura Best
- Staff: Marie Barber, Ann Bear, Areta Bingham, Kass Burchett, Rebecca Christensen, Holly Fuller, Marilyn Goff, Shirley Heslop, Holly Hollingsworth, Shawn Hsu, Susan Jorgensen, Leslie Liechty, Pauline Locke, Ginger Mikkelsen, Barbara Milburn, Linda Orton, Karmen Quinney, Rhonda Rainey, Leslie Ridenour, and Cindy Stoeckl

Plaid Enterprises:

- Editor: Mickey Baskett
- Staff: Jeff Herr, Laney McClure, Susan Mickey, Dianne Miller, Jerry Mucklow, Phyllis Mueller, and Suzanne Yoder

If you have any questions or comments or would like information on specialty products featured in this book, please contact: Chapelle, Ltd., Inc., P.O. Box 9252, Ogden, UT 84409 • (801) 621-2777 • (801) 621-2788 Fax

Library of Congress Cataloging-in-Publication Data

Painted birdhouses / Plaid.
    p.   cm.
    "A Sterling/Chapelle book".
    Includes index.
    ISBN 0-8069-1345-2
    1. Painting.   2. Decoration and ornament. 3. Birdhouses.
 I.   Plaid Enterprises.
TT385.P34 1998
745.7'23--DC21
                                           98-14776
                                             CIP

"A Sterling/Chapelle Book"

10 9 8 7 6 5 4 3 2 1

Published by Sterling Publishing Company, Inc.
387 Park Avenue South, New York, NY 10016
©1998 by Chapelle Ltd.
Distributed in Canada by Sterling Publishing
c/o Canadian Manda Group, One Atlantic Avenue, Suite 105
Toronto, Ontario, Canada M6K 3E7
Distributed in Great Britain and Europe by Cassell PLC
Wellington House, 125 Strand
London WCR2 0BB, England
Distributed in Australia by Capricorn Link (Australia) Pty Ltd.
P.O. Box 6651, Baulkham Hills, Business Centre
NSW 2153, Australia

Printed in the United States of America

Sterling ISBN 0-8069-1345-2

Contents

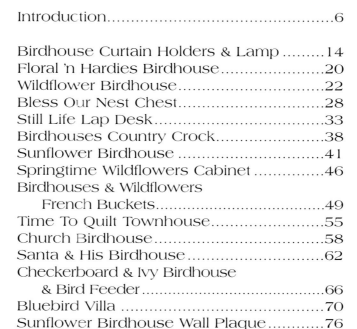

Introduction

ACRYLIC PAINTS

Acrylic Craft Paints:

Acrylic craft paints are richly pigmented flat finish paints. They are packaged in bottles and available in a huge range of colors. They are ready to use, with no mixing required. Simply squeeze paints from bottle onto palette and begin painting. Because they are water-based, acrylic paints dry quickly and cleanup is easy.

Artist Pigment Acrylic Paints:

This palette of pure, intense, universal pigment colors is true to the nature of standard pigments. Because of the pure pigmentation, these colors can be intermixed to achieve true colors. They can also be intermixed and used in conjunction with acrylic craft paints.

Acrylic Gloss Enamels:

These gloss finish enamels are weather resistant and durable. They can be used indoors or outdoors. Their bright, intense colors allow for an opaque coverage.

Metallic Acrylic Craft Paints:

These metallic paints add luxurious luster and iridescence to surfaces and can be used with any other acrylic paints.

ACRYLIC PAINTING MEDIUMS

Acrylic painting mediums can be used with paint to create certain effects or change the paint's performance without affecting the paint color.

Blending Gel Mediums:

Apply blending gel mediums to areas before painting to increase drying time and make it easy to smoothly blend colors.

Extenders:

Extenders are used to increase drying time and become transparent when floating, blending, and washing colors. They are also used to create effects without color reduction.

Thickeners:

Thickeners should be mixed with paint to create transparent color while maintaining a thick and consistent flow.

Textile Mediums:

To create permanent, washable painted effects on fabric, mix textile mediums with acrylic paint. The textile medium allows the paint to penetrate fibers and retain softness so fabrics are not stiff.

Unfinished Wood:

Sand new wood with medium (150 grit) sandpaper in the direction of the grain. Wipe away dust with a soft cloth or a tack cloth. Base paint, let dry, and sand with fine (220 grit) sandpaper. Apply a second coat of base color. Let dry.

Painted Wood:

Sand painted wood with medium (150 grit) sandpaper until surface feels smooth. Wipe away paint particles with a soft cloth or a tack cloth. It is not necessary to remove all the old paint.

Metal:

Galvanized tin has an oily film that must be removed before painting. To wipe clean, use a sponge or cloth and a solution of three parts water to one part vinegar. Do not immerse piece in water as the water can become trapped in areas of the piece causing problems later. Dry piece thoroughly before painting.

Painted or enameled tin requires damp sponging with water and drying.

Old tin should be rubbed with steel wool and wiped with a tack cloth.

When painting tinware, do not overstroke. Overstroking has a tendency to pull up layers of paint. Load brush well enough to make one continuous stroke. Tinware pieces are very susceptible to scratching. Handle your painted piece very carefully until sealer has been applied.

Floating Mediums:

Floating mediums are used instead of water for floating, shading, and highlighting. Floating mediums do not run like water, offering more control, and they do not contain extenders, so drying time is not increased.

FINISHES

Aerosol Finishes:

Aerosol finishes are sprayed on painted surfaces to seal and protect against moisture, soil, and dust. They dry clear and are non-yellowing. Gloss sealers dry with a gloss finish. Matte sealers dry with a matte finish.

Waterbase Varnishes:

This brush-on liquid finish protects and seals surfaces and dries with a satin finish. It also offers excellent resistance to scratches and water spotting.

OTHER SUPPLIES

- Brush cleaner — for cleaning and conditioning brushes.
- Palette — for arranging and mixing paints.
- Palette knife — for mixing paints.
- Paper towels — for wiping brushes and for cleanup.
- Sandpaper — for removing burrs and rough spots from wood.
- Tack cloth — for removing sanding dust from wood.
- Tracing paper — for tracing patterns.
- Water basin — for rinsing brushes.

(See individual project instructions for additional supplies needed.)

7

Fabric:

Wash and dry fabric according to manufacturer's directions before painting to remove sizing and excess dye and guard against shrinkage after painting. Do not use fabric softener.

Terra-cotta and Clay Pots:

Wash terra-cotta and clay pots with water and mild soap. Allow them to dry thoroughly before painting.

Transferring Patterns:

Many of the patterns for the projects in this book have been reduced in order to give you the maximum number of patterns possible. You will need to enlarge them on a photocopier according to the percentages given, or adjust the size to accommodate your painting surface.

To keep your book intact, trace main lines of the pattern on tracing paper. Position the traced design on the painting surface and tape one edge with masking tape. Slide transfer paper underneath tracing paper and lightly trace pattern lines with a stylus. Add details as you paint by following the pattern or project photograph.

BRUSHES

There are no set rules for choosing brushes — try a variety of styles and qualities and make your own choices.

The quality of the brush is important to the success of the painting. Quality brushes bend easily, then return to their original shape. In general, use the best quality brush you can afford.

Brushes are made from either synthetics or animal hair. Synthetic brushes are made especially for use with acrylic paints.

Many brushes are designed for a specific purpose:

• Flat brushes are used for basecoating, sideloading, and floating. Flat brushes have long hairs and a chisel edge. The size of the brush to be used is determined by the size of the detail to be painted.

• Shaders are flat brushes with short hairs and a chisel edge. The size of the brush to be used is determined by the size of the detail to be painted.

• Deerfoot brushes or old flat brushes are used for stippling.

• Round brushes have a fine point for delicate lines and detail work. The size of the brush to be used is determined by the size of the detail to be painted.

• For small detail, liners or script liners are used. Script liners hold more paint for long, continuous strokes.

• Mop brushes are used for blending.

• Sponge brushes are used for basecoating.

• Stencil brushes or old toothbrushes are used for spattering or flyspecking.

• Filbert brushes are used for making teardrop shapes.

• Angle shaders are used for floating.

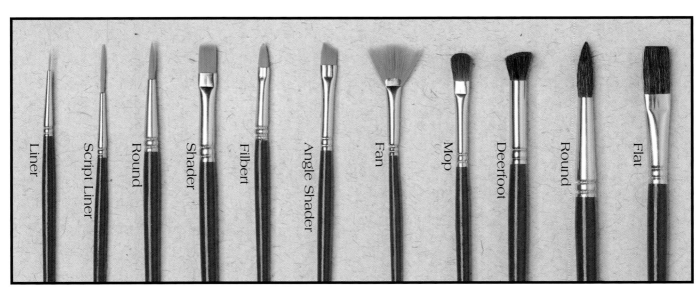

Liner · Script Liner · Round · Shader · Filbert · Angle Shader · Fan · Mop · Deerfoot · Round · Flat

BRUSH CARE

Cleaning brushes thoroughly after each use is extremely important. Rinse bristles in water, then clean with a good brush cleaner. Rinse thoroughly and reshape wet bristles to a flat shape (for flats or shaders) or pointed shape (for rounds and liners). Let dry. Before painting again, rinse bristles well.

BASIC PAINTING TERMS

Base-coat:
To fill in design completely with a solid coat of color. Paint with as few strokes as possible. Shade and highlight on top of the basecoat.

C-stroke:
Paint a "C" using one stroke of the brush. The stroke size depends on the design.

Dot:
Dip the end of a brush handle or a stylus in paint and press on surface to make dots for berries, flowers, etc.

Double load:
Load two colors, one on each half of the brush. When reloading, keep the same color on the same half of the brush each time.

Dry brush:
Dip brush into a tiny bit of paint and blot on a paper towel to remove excess paint. Lightly brush paint on project.

Float:
Floating is used for shading and highlighting. Dampen area to be floated with water. Sideload brush and apply paint to dampened area. Do not over-work area. Allow to dry thoroughly before refloating. You may need to apply two or three floats before shading is dark enough or highlights are bright enough. Make the first float the widest and each successive float narrower.

Highlight:
Add dimension by adding light colors making an area seem closer. Load brush with extender, sideload with highlight color, and apply to design.

Inky:
Mix paint with water until the paint is the consistency of ink. When loading brush, roll paint off to tip. Test to see if there's enough paint on brush.

Load:
Stroke brush back and forth in paint or medium until brush is full.

Shade:
Shading creates shadows, darkens and deepens color, and makes an area recede. To shade, load brush with extender, sideload with shading color, and apply to design.

Sideload:
Load brush with paint. Pick up another color for shading on one edge of brush. When sideloading for floating, dip a flat brush in water and blot once on a paper towel. Load only left corner of brush with paint. Stroke brush back and forth on palette until paint gradually blends into water. No paint should be on right corner of the brush.

Spatter:
This technique is used to obtain an antique look and add color and character. Using a stencil brush or old toothbrush, dip bristles into water. Blot on a paper towel to remove excess water. Dip brush into paint, working paint into bristles by tapping on palette. Point brush toward area to be spattered and pull your thumb across bristles to flip top of bristles and send "spatters" or "flyspecks" of paint onto project.

Stipple:
Dab a deerfoot brush or stencil brush in paint. If project instructions call for stippling with more than one color, pick up both colors on brush. Blot brush once or twice on a paper towel to get a good blend, then pounce up and down on surface.

Walk:
When floating color, "walk" or gradually move brush from left to right or right to left.

Wash:
This transparent layer of paint over a base color is four parts paint to one part water or medium. Load brush and use long strokes on the surface.

Wet on Wet:
While paint is still wet, pick up shading or highlighting color on brush and paint area, blending new color into previous one.

BRUSH STROKE TECHNIQUES

Loading with Flat Brush:
Touch brush into paint at a 45° angle, then gently pull away. Load all the way across chisel edge of brush. Try not to apply too much pressure when loading. Load no more than ¾ of the way up the fibers.

Double-Loading with Flat Brush:
Full-load first color onto brush. Then sideload second color. Continue to gently pull paint away in the same spot to completely blend dark and light values, creating a middle value.

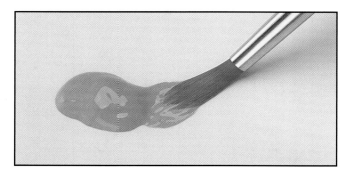

Loading with Round Brush:
Touch brush into paint, then gently pull away. Brush is at a lower angle to load, therefore the paint can go all the way up to the ferrule.

Sideloading with Flat Brush:
To thin paint, dampen brush with water or extender. Touch one side of brush into paint, then gently pull away. Place corner of brush on top of pulled-down paint and pull gently away. Repeat until desired color is on one side of brush and color dissipates toward the opposite side.

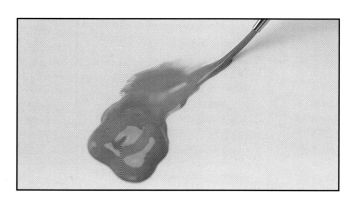

Loading with Script Liner:
To thin paint, dampen brush with water or extender. Load brush with paint up to the ferrule, then gently pull away.

Tips and Techniques Worksheet

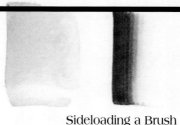

Sideloading a Brush

Wash
Thin paint with water. This technique works great for skies and ground.

Wrong
Too much water. Paint went all the way across brush.

Wrong
Not enough water. Left a hard line.

Right
Gradual change from paint to clear water.

Floating
To widen a floated area, walk brush across, overlapping each stroke.

Float a wide cheek area. Let dry.

To intensify, float again, only not as wide. Repeat as many times as needed.

Stippling
Use a deerfoot or stencil brush. Pounce darkest color or value. Let dry.

Pounce second color or medium value. Let dry.

Pounce highlight color or lightest value. Be careful not to lose your dark and medium values.

Descending Dots
Dip brush handle into paint. Dot 3 or 4 times before redipping into paint. Always use fresh paint when making dots.

Same Size Dots
Dip brush hancle into paint before making each dot.

Folk Art Hearts

Make one dot.

Redip brush handle and place a second dot next to the first dot.

Using a liner or the small end of a stylus, pull the point down from the dots.

Simple Brush Strokes

Comma stroke
with flat brush

S-stroke
with flat brush

Comma stroke start
with round brush

Comma stroke end
with round brush

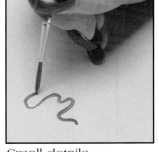

Small details
with liner or
script liner

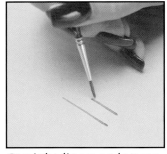

Straight lines or letters
with liner brush

Ruffles
with angle shader

Petals
with angle shader

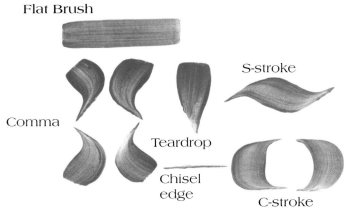

Flat Brush

Comma

S-stroke

Teardrop

Chisel
edge

C-stroke

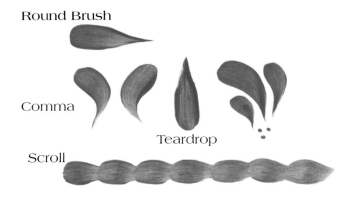

Round Brush

Comma

Teardrop

Scroll

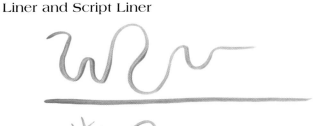

Liner and Script Liner

Angle Shader

Ruffle

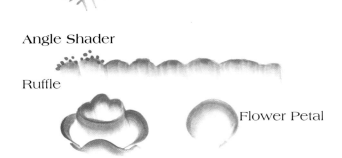

Flower Petal

Start of comma
stroke with
filbert brush

End of comma stroke
with filbert brush,
lift and turn

Patting motion
with deerfoot brush

Making grass with
deerfoot brush

Making dots for
hearts with
brush handle

Blending cr
softening color
with mop brush

Checkerboards
with sponge

Squares
with sponge

Filbert Brush

Stencil Brush

Stenciling   Spattering

Deerfoot Brush

Patting   Fur

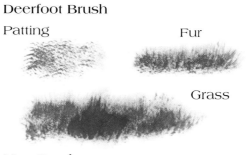

Grass

Mop Brush

Softening Edges or Blending

Handle End of Brush

Dots   Dot Flower

Dot Heart

Sponge

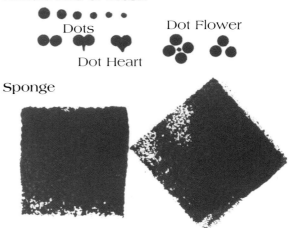

Square   Check

13

Birdhouse Curtain Holders & Lamp
Instructions begin on page 15

Birdhouse Curtain Holders & Lamp

Pictured on pages 14 & 16

Designed by
Dianna Marcum

These pieces are, not only fun, but quick to make and they look great in just about any room.

GATHER THESE SUPPLIES

Painting Surfaces:
Wooden birdhouse
   curtain holders (2)
Wooden birdhouse lamp
Wooden bird, approx. 2½" long

Paints, Stains, and Finishes:
Acrylic craft paints:
   Almond Parfait
   Blue Ribbon
   Burnt Umber
   Coffee Bean
   Licorice
   Napthol Crimson
   Promenade Coral
   Tapioca
   Thicket
   Yellow Ochre
Antiquing medium:
   Apple Butter Brown
Waterbase varnish
Matte spray sealer

Brushes:
Angle shaders
Old toothbrush
Round brush
Script liner
Sponge brushes
Stencil brush or small sponge

Other Supplies:
Lampshade, 7½" tall,
   11" diameter at bottom
Fabric: floral print for
   lampshade, ½ yd.;
   coordinating fabrics for
   curtains and lining
Coordinating thread
Double-stick adhesive
Hand-sewing needle
Iron & ironing board
Marking tool
Newspaper
Sandpaper
Scissors
Sewing machine
Stencils: ¾" heart; 1¼" heart

Optional: Braid or other trim and fabric glue

INSTRUCTIONS

Prepare and Base-coat:
1. Prepare wood. See Surface Preparation on page 7.

2. Paint birdhouses with Almond Parfait. Paint roofs and rims of lamp base with Thicket. Paint lamp pole with Coffee Bean. Paint chimney with Napthol Crimson. Paint bird with Tapioca. Let dry.

3. Transfer details from Birdhouse Curtain Holder Pattern on page 18 onto curtain holders. Transfer details from Birdhouse Lamp Base Pattern on page 19 onto lamp. Transfer details from Birdhouse Lamp Bird Pattern on page 19 onto bird.

PAINT THE DESIGN

Stenciled Hearts:
1. Stencil a 1¼" heart at upper front of lamp birdhouse with Napthol Crimson, using a stencil brush or a small sponge.

2. Stencil a ¾" heart at upper front of each curtain holder birdhouse.

Bird:
1. Float Promenade Coral on bird tummy.

2. Float Blue Ribbon along wings and upper body.

3. Paint beak with Yellow Ochre. Float a bit of Coffee Bean on beak close to head.

4. Add a Coffee Bean dot for an eye on each side.

Vines:
1. Paint vines with thinned Coffee Bean. Keep it pretty loose — don't try to make it perfect. Add some darker vines with thinned Burnt Umber. Also use Burnt Umber to shade a few vines making them appear to be underneath others.

2. Paint berries with Napthol Crimson dots. When dry, add a tiny Tapioca highlight to each.

3. Paint flower petals with dots of Blue Ribbon. Add a Yellow Ochre dot to the center of each. Paint leaves with Thicket.

FINISH

Wood Pieces:
1. When dry, sand the edges of the pieces, including the bird.

2. Spray with two coats of matte spray sealer.

Continued on page 17

Continued from page 15

3. Spatter all areas, including bird, with thinned Burnt Umber and thinned Licorice. Let dry.

4. Apply two coats of waterbase varnish. Let dry.

5. Antique with Apple Butter Brown, wiping off excess. Let dry.

6. Finish with two additional coats of waterbase varnish. Let dry.

7. Install curtain holders on window.

Lampshade:

1. Lay lampshade on a large piece of newspaper. Using the lampshade as a template, roll it along and use a marking tool to follow bottom onto the newspaper as you roll. Repeat for top. Cut out along marked lines. Check to see if newspaper pattern fits shade.

2. Follow manufacturer's directions for applying double-stick adhesive to the wrong side of fabric.

3. Lay newspaper pattern on fabric. Cut out 1" larger than pattern on all sides.

4. Remove paper backing and smooth fabric in place on lampshade. Either: Clip into the fabric margins around the shade, then press the raw edges to the inside of shade or trim edges even with bottom and top of shade.

Optional: Glue braid or other trim around top and bottom of lampshade to cover the edges.

Curtains:

Note: To determine amount of fabric needed for curtains and lining, measure width of window plus amount to hang down plus 2 feet for draping. Add even more for a large window. Buy an equal amount of fabric for lining.

1. Before sewing, drape fabric through holders on window to see exactly how much fabric is needed. You may need to seam the fabric to obtain the length you need. If so, try to position the seams inside the birdhouse holders (or match the seams well enough that the piecing does not show.)

2. Place curtain and lining fabrics with right sides together. Sew around outer edges, leaving an opening for turning.

3. Turn right sides out. Hand-stitch the opening closed. Press all edges.

4. Drape curtains around window through curtain holders.

Floral 'n Hardies Birdhouse

Pictured on page 20

Designed by
Pat Wakefield

Cutouts from seed catalogs are glued to this rustic birdhouse and embellished with painted flowers and greenery.

GATHER THESE SUPPLIES

Painting Surface:
Birdhouse, 4½" x 4½" x 12" high

Paints, Stains, and Finishes:
Acrylic craft paints:
Apple Spice
Charcoal Gray
Emerald Isle
Grass Green
Hot Pink
Licorice
Light Periwinkle
Maple Syrup
Poppy Red
Raw Umber
Tangerine
Warm White
Yellow Light
Acrylic painting medium:
extender
Waterbase varnish

Brushes:
Flat brushes
Liner
Mop brush
Round brushes

Other Supplies:
Pencil
Sandpaper
Scissors
Soft cloth
Variety of seed catalogs
White craft glue

INSTRUCTIONS

Prepare and Base-coat:
1. Prepare wood. See Surface Preparation on page 7.

2. Paint front, back, and sides of birdhouse with Light Periwinkle. Paint roof with Charcoal Gray. Let dry.

3. Sand entire piece to remove some of the paint,
Continued on page 21

Birdhouse Curtain Holder Pattern

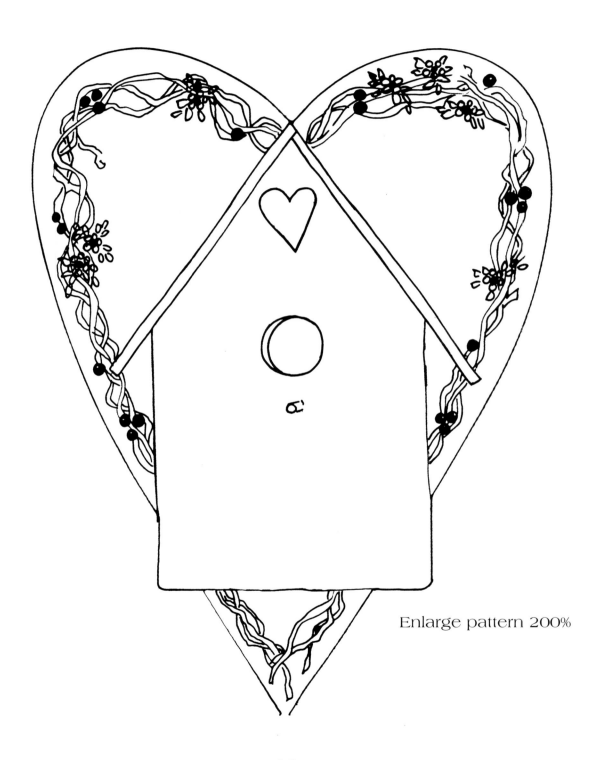

Enlarge pattern 200%

Birdhouse Lamp Bird Pattern

Pattern is actual size

Birdhouse Lamp Base Pattern

Pattern is actual size

Floral 'n Hardies Birdhouse
Instructions begin on page 17

Plant Foods
and Fertilizers

Deluxe Iris Collection

FLORAL
'N
HARDIES

Lime

Crabgrass Preventer
Plus Lawn Food

GARDENS®

SPECIAL
VALUES

Continued from page 17

especially on edges of the house and the roof.

4. Thin Raw Umber with water or extender. Paint over entire piece providing an antique look. Use a cloth to wipe off excess.

Add Cutouts:
1. Cut out small signs, trees, bunches of flowers, or bushes from seed catalogs.

2. Using a pencil, very lightly draw windows, shutters, and doors on the house.

3. Arrange cutouts around sides and roof. Glue in place.

4. Using thin wash of Raw Umber, antique over cutouts.

PAINT THE DESIGN

1. Embellish cutouts by extending leaves and flowers with ones you have painted. Use Grass Green and Emerald Isle for leaves. Add lighter leaves with Grass Green mixed with Yellow Light.

2. For flowers, use a variety of bright paint colors from your palette. Paint small dots to resemble blossoms.

3. Paint windows with Licorice. Add window trim with Light Periwinkle.

4. Paint shutters and window boxes with Apple Spice.

5. Paint hanging flower pots with Warm White or Maple Syrup.

6. Add leaves and flowers in flower pots with dots of bright colors.

FINISH

1. Apply two coats of water-base varnish.

Wildflower Birdhouse

Pictured on page 22

Designed by
Donna Dewberry

These painting techniques are very easy to accomplish with worksheets giving detailed painting instructions.

GATHER THESE SUPPLIES

Painting Surface:
Wooden birdhouse,
    7" x 7½" x 8" high

Paints, Stains, and Finishes:
Acrylic craft paints:
    Berry Wine
    Country Twill
    Dark Brown
    Dioxazine Purple
    Green Forest
    Midnight
    Wicker White
Matte spray sealer

Brushes:
Deerfoot brush
Flat brushes
Script liner

INSTRUCTIONS

Prepare and Base-coat:
1. Prepare wood. See Surface Preparation on page 7.

2. Paint birdhouse and perch with two coats of Wicker White. Paint roof with Midnight. Let dry.

PAINT THE DESIGN

1. Using a flat brush double-loaded with Wicker White and Country Twill, paint vertical streaks on walls to look like boards.

2. Using a flat brush double-loaded with Midnight and Wicker White, paint roof shingles.

3. Paint crosshatching on front edge of roof with Wicker White. Let dry.

4. Transfer Wildflower Birdhouse Roof Pattern on page 26 to roof of birdhouse. Transfer Wildflower Birdhouse Back Pattern on page 27 to back of birdhouse. Transfer Wildflower Birdhouse Front & Sides Pattern on page 23 to front and sides of birdhouse.

5. Paint heart with Berry Wine mixed with Wicker White.

6. Paint bows with Dioxazine Purple.

7. Using a script liner, paint lettering with Berry Wine.

8. Paint flowers, topiaries, vines, and grass, using Wildflower Birdhouse Worksheets on pages 24 and 25. Let dry.

FINISH

1. Spray with two coats of matte spray sealer.

Wildflower Birdhouse Front & Sides Pattern

Enlarge pattern 175%

Welcome

Wildflower Birdhouse Worksheets

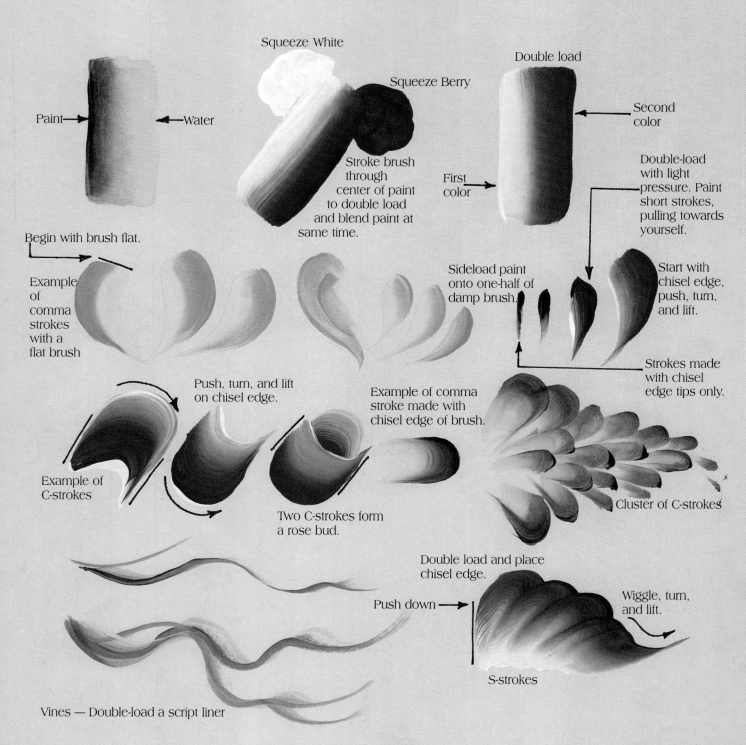

Paint→ ←Water

Squeeze White

Squeeze Berry

Stroke brush through center of paint to double load and blend paint at same time.

Double load

Second color

First color

Double-load with light pressure. Paint short strokes, pulling towards yourself.

Begin with brush flat.

Example of comma strokes with a flat brush

Sideload paint onto one-half of damp brush.

Start with chisel edge, push, turn, and lift.

Push, turn, and lift on chisel edge.

Example of comma stroke made with chisel edge of brush.

Strokes made with chisel edge tips only.

Example of C-strokes

Two C-strokes form a rose bud.

Cluster of C-strokes

Double load and place chisel edge.

Push down →

Wiggle, turn, and lift.

S-strokes

Vines — Double-load a script liner

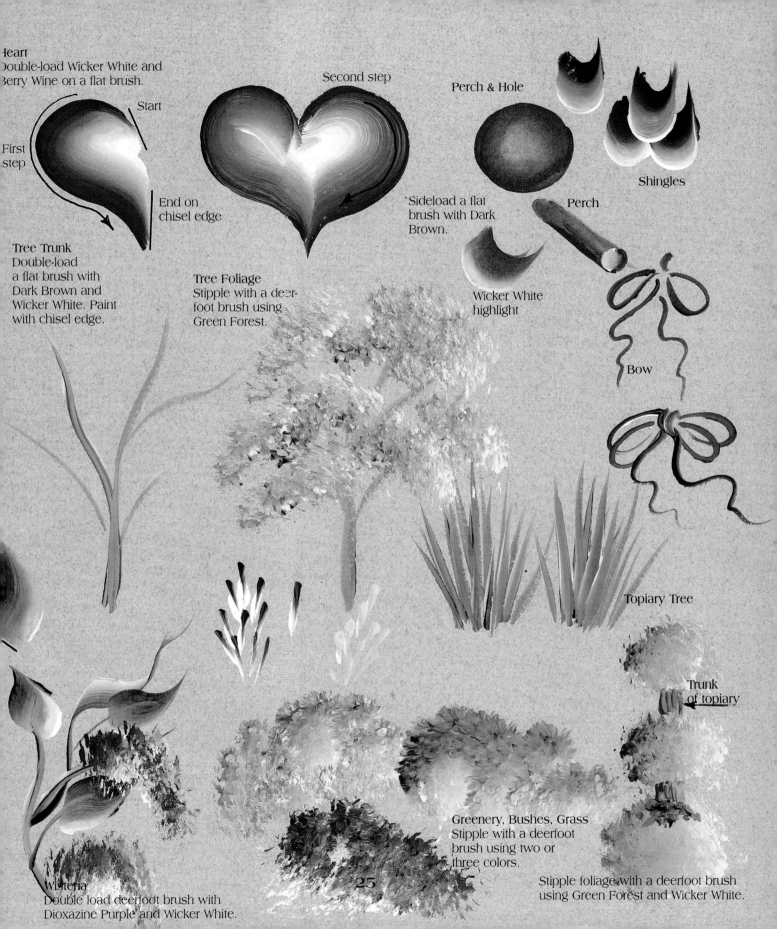

Heart
Double-load Wicker White and Berry Wine on a flat brush.

Start

First step

Second step

End on chisel edge

Perch & Hole

Shingles

Perch

Sideload a flat brush with Dark Brown.

Wicker White highlight

Bow

Tree Trunk
Double-load a flat brush with Dark Brown and Wicker White. Paint with chisel edge.

Tree Foliage
Stipple with a deerfoot brush using Green Forest.

Topiary Tree

Trunk of topiary

Greenery, Bushes, Grass
Stipple with a deerfoot brush using two or three colors.

Wisteria
Double load deerfoot brush with Dioxazine Purple and Wicker White.

25

Stipple foliage with a deerfoot brush using Green Forest and Wicker White.

Wildflower Birdhouse Roof Pattern

Center of Roof

Pattern is actual size

Wildflower Birdhouse Back Pattern

Pattern is actual size

Bless Our Nest Chest
Instructions begin on page 29

Bless Our Nest Chest

Pictured on page 28

Designed by
Sue Bailey

An array of fanciful bird-houses adorns the top of this wooden chest. This pattern would also be wonderful on a console table or on a plaque.

Use as many of the houses as you wish, adapting the width of the design to fit your project.

GATHER THESE SUPPLIES

Painting Surface:
Wooden chest,
    18" x 9½" x 10" high

Paints, Stains, and Finishes:
Acrylic craft paints:
    Burnt Sienna
    Burnt Umber
    Hunter Green
    Ivory Black
    Napthol Crimson
    Navy Blue
    Poppy Red
    Raw Sienna
    Red Light
    True Blue
    Wicker White
    Yellow Medium
Oil paint: Burnt Umber
Waterbase varnish
Wood stain: Early American

Brushes:
Flat brushes
Script liner
Sponge brush

Other Supplies:
Mineral spirits
Masking tape
Paper
Permanent black ink pen
Ruler
Soft cloth or rag
Transfer tool

INSTRUCTIONS

Prepare and Base-coat:
1. Prepare wood. See Surface Preparation on page 7.

2. Stain chest base, edge of lid, and inside with Early American.

3. Paint top of lid and sides of chest with two coats Wicker White. Let dry.

4. Measure 1" from edge around top of lid. Tape on inside (where the pattern will be). With a soft cloth or rag, apply Burnt Umber oil paint, starting at tape and rubbing over paint to the outer edge.

5. Apply mineral spirits to cloth or rag and rub to remove more oil paint to give an antique look. Let dry.

6. Trace Bless Our Nest Chest Pattern on page 30 on paper and place on front of chest. Hold pattern with one hand and, with the other hand, apply Burnt Umber oil paint with a cloth or rag over the remainder of the front, stroking from the oval out to the sides. Then rub with mineral spirits. Use the same technique on remaining sides.

7. Mask off thin brown border ⅛" wide with tape. (This takes a little time, but the lines will be straight.) Paint with Burnt Umber acrylic paint. Let dry. Remove tape.

8. Trace and transfer Bless Our Nest Chest Top Pattern on page 31 onto top of chest.

PAINT THE DESIGN

Fence:
1. Using a ruler and the black ink pen, outline the fence.

2. Shade stringers (the horizontal boards) with Ivory Black mixed with Wicker White.

Leaves and Vines:
1. Paint leaves and vines with Hunter Green. Add a little Burnt Umber mixed with Hunter Green to some leaves for variation.

2. Letter "Bless Our Nest" with two coats of Burnt Umber acrylic paint.

Birds:
1. Three Bluebirds: Paint head, back, wings, and tail with True Blue. Highlight with True Blue mixed with Wicker White. Paint breast with Poppy Red mixed with Wicker White.

2. Two Yellow Birds: Base with Yellow Medium. Shade with Burnt Sienna. Highlight with Wicker White. Detail and outline with black ink pen.

3. Two Brown Birds: Base with Raw Sienna. Highlight with Wicker White.

4. Eyes for Blue, Yellow, and Brown Birds: Dot with Ivory Black. Add a smaller dot of Wicker White.

5. One Red Bird: Base with Red Light. Paint beak and

mask with Ivory Black. Dot eye with Wicker White and add detail with black ink pen.

6. Black Bird: Base with Ivory Black. Highlight with Wicker White. Dot eye with Wicker White.

7. Paint all birds' legs and feet with Ivory Black. Highlight with Wicker White.

8. Paint beaks with Ivory Black. Highlight with Wicker White.

Birdhouses:
Note: Instructions are given in order of left to right.

1. Paint the blue cottage.
a. Base with True Blue. Add Wicker White to True Blue and lighten front.
b. Paint door and holes with Ivory Black; highlight with Wicker White.
c. Paint roof with Raw Sienna; streak with streaks of Wicker White. Paint chimney with Burnt Sienna; paint bricks with Wicker White.
d. Paint base with Raw Sienna; add Wicker White to Raw Sienna to lighten front. Shade underneath base and paint pole with Burnt Umber.

2. Paint the red cottage.
a. Base with Poppy Red. Add Wicker White to Poppy Red to lighten front.
b. Paint hole and perch with Ivory Black; highlight with Wicker White.
c. Paint roof, base, and pole with Ivory Black; highlight with Wicker White.

3. Paint the green cottage.
a. Base with Hunter Green. Add Wicker White to Hunter Green to lighten front. Add lines of Ivory Black to front.
b. Paint hole and perch with Ivory Black; highlight with Wicker White.
c. Paint base with Raw Sienna; add Wicker White to front to lighten. Shade underneath base and paint pole with Burnt Umber; highlight with Wicker White.

4. Paint Noah's Ark.
a. Base hull with Raw Sienna; highlight with Wicker White. Outline and paint board lines, holes, and perch with Ivory Black. Highlight holes with Wicker White.
b. Paint water with True Blue; highlight with Wicker White.
c. Paint cabin walls with Red Light; shade with Red Light mixed with Ivory Black. Paint

board lines with Ivory Black. Paint hole with Ivory Black; highlight with Wicker White.
d. Paint roof with Ivory Black; highlight with Wicker White. Paint pole with Raw Sienna.

5. Paint the lighthouse:
a. Paint top, stripes, and base with Navy Blue. Shade on each side with gray (Ivory Black mixed with Wicker White). Dry-brush with Wicker White down center.
b. Paint window with Ivory Black. Paint door with Ivory Black mixed with Wicker White. Paint walkways with Ivory Black; highlight with Wicker White mixed with Yellow Medium.
c. Paint top ball with Raw Sienna; highlight with Wicker White.
d. Paint observation window with Poppy Red mixed with

Continued on page 32

Bless Our Nest Chest Pattern

Enlarge pattern 125%

Bless Our Nest Chest

Top Pattern

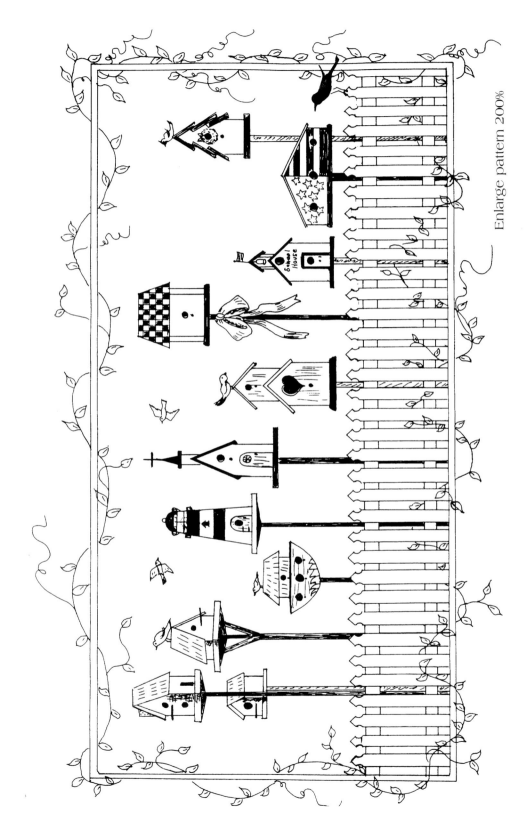

Enlarge pattern 200%

Continued from page 30

Wicker White. Add in a little True Blue and some Wicker White to suggest clouds. Paint light in center of observation area with Yellow Medium mixed with Wicker White. Paint trim on observation area with Ivory Black; highlight with Wicker White.
e. Shade underneath and paint pole with Burnt Umber; highlight with Wicker White.

6. Paint church.
a. Outline with Ivory Black.
b. Paint top, roof, door, hole, perch, and base with Ivory Black. Highlight inside the hole and add lines of Wicker White on door.
c. Paint stained glass with True Blue mixed with Wicker White, Poppy Red mixed with White, and Yellow Medium mixed with Wicker White. Separate with Ivory Black.

7. Paint barn.
a. Base with Napthol Crimson. Shade with Napthol Crimson mixed with Ivory Black. Paint board lines with Ivory Black. Highlight with Wicker White.
b. Paint inside hole and heart with Ivory Black. Highlight with Wicker White.
c. Paint roof with Napthol Crimson mixed with Wicker White.
d. Paint base and pole with Ivory Black. Highlight with Wicker White.

8. Paint checkerboard cottage.
a. Outline roof with Ivory Black. Paint every other square with Ivory Black, using photo as a guide.
b. Paint walls with two coats Hunter Green. Add Wicker White to Hunter Green on corner posts. Add board lines with Ivory Black.
c. Paint hole and perch with Ivory Black. Highlight with Wicker White.
d. Paint base with Ivory Black. Highlight with Wicker White.
e. Paint pole with Burnt Umber. Highlight with Wicker White.
f. Base bow with Yellow Medium. Shade with Burnt Sienna. Highlight with Wicker White.

9. Paint school house.
a. Base walls and cupola posts with two coats Napthol Crimson. Shade with Napthol Crimson mixed with Ivory Black.
b. Paint sides, trim around door, hole, lettering, roofs, and base with Ivory Black. Highlight with Wicker White.
c. Paint bell with Yellow Medium. Shade with Burnt Sienna. Highlight with Wicker White.
d. Paint stripes on flag with Napthol Crimson. Paint square with Navy Blue. Make dots with Wicker White for stars.
e. Paint flag pole and pole with Ivory Black.

10. Paint flag house.
a. Paint left side with Navy Blue. Highlight with Wicker White. Paint stars with Wicker White.
b. Paint stripes on right side with Napthol Crimson.
c. Paint holes with Ivory Black. Highlight with Wicker White.
d. Paint roof and base with Ivory Black. Highlight with Wicker White.
e. Paint pole with Burnt Umber. Highlight with Wicker White.

11. Paint Christmas cottage.
a. Outline with Ivory Black.
b. Paint roof, base, pole, and wreath around hole with Hunter Green. Highlight with Wicker White.
c. Paint perch and hole with Ivory Black. Highlight with Wicker White.
d. Paint bow on wreath with Red Light. Highlight with Wicker White. Let dry.

FINISH

1. Apply waterbase varnish.

Still Life Lap Desk

Pictured on page 33

Designed by
Sue Bailey

Birds, birdhouses, sunflowers, and apples create a colorful still life. The checked border is echoed on the green birdhouse roof. If you love birdhouses, this scene would be fun to paint on a variety of surfaces such as wooden trays, plaques, and small tabletops.

GATHER THESE SUPPLIES

Painting Surface:
Wooden lap desk

Paints, Stains, and Finishes:
Acrylic craft paints:
    Burnt Sienna
    Burnt Umber
    Dark Gray
    Hunter Green
    Ivory Black
    Light Gray
    Medium Gray
Continued on page 34

Still Life Lap Desk
Instructions begin on page 32

Continued from page 32

Napthol Crimson
Raw Sienna
Red Light
Sunflower
True Blue
Wicker White
Yellow Medium
Waterbase varnish
Wood stain: Early American

Brushes:
Deerfoot brush
Flat brushes
Script liner
Sponge brush

Other Supplies:
Sea sponge
Permanent black ink pen
Masking tape

INSTRUCTIONS

Prepare and Base-coat:
1. Remove hinges and lid. Prepare wood. See Surface Preparation on page 7.

2. Stain lap desk, except the top of the lid with Early American.

3. Paint handle with Ivory Black.

4. Dampen sea sponge. Squeeze out excess water. Sponge top of lid with Wicker White and Wicker White mixed with Sunflower. Let dry.

5. Tape off checked borders. Base with Wicker White. Let dry.

6. Tape off checks. Paint with Ivory Black. Let dry.

7. Transfer Still Life Lap Desk Pattern on page 36.

PAINT THE DESIGN

Paint Brushes:
1. Base brown handled brushes with Raw Sienna. Shade with Burnt Umber. Highlight with Raw Sienna mixed with Wicker White.

2. Base black handled brush with Ivory Black. Highlight with Wicker White.

3. Base metal shanks with Medium Gray. Add a line down the center of shanks and handles with Wicker White.

4. Paint bristles with Raw Sienna. Shade with Burnt Umber.

5. Add Red Light on end of one brush. Add Hunter Green to another. Add True Blue to remaining brush. Highlight all with Wicker White.

6. Outline brushes with Ivory Black. Shade under brushes with Burnt Umber.

Bluebirds:
There are five birds with blue backs and two with brown backs.

1. Paint brown back birds.
a. Paint backs with Burnt Umber and Burnt Umber mixed with Wicker White.
b. Paint breasts, starting at beak and working down, with Burnt Sienna mixed with Red Light and Sunflower mixed with Wicker White, using choppy strokes. Add a little Burnt Umber on the breast toward the tail.
c. Add True Blue mixed with Wicker White on the wings.

2. Paint blue back birds.
a. Base heads, backs, wings, and tails with True Blue.
b. Paint breasts with Burnt Sienna mixed with Red Light and Wicker White, using choppy strokes.
c. Highlight heads, wings, and tail with True Blue mixed with Wicker White. With Wicker White on a liner brush, pull comma strokes on wings and tails.

3. Paint beaks, legs, feet, and eyes with Ivory Black. Highlight with Wicker White. Add a line of Wicker White under each eye.

4. Paint straw in the mouth of Bird on jar with Raw Sienna. Highlight with Wicker White.

Napkin on Table:
1. Base with Wicker White. Shade with Dark Gray, floating color under the pan, around flowers, and in folds of the scarf. Highlight with Wicker White.

2. Paint trim lines with the Red Light.

Apple Butter Jar:
1. Base lid with Light Gray. Shade with Dark Gray. Highlight with Wicker White.

2. To paint apple butter, dab on Burnt Umber mixed with Raw Sienna, Raw Sienna mixed with Yellow Medium, and Raw Sienna mixed with Wicker White very loosely, using chisel edge of the brush. Leave an open area at top of jar.

3. Shade under lid with a Dark Gray floating color.

4. Highlight jar with strokes of Wicker White, using chisel edge of brush. Add a tint of Red Light next to apples.

5. Paint inner area of label with Wicker White. Paint edges with Red Light. Shade next to pan with Red Light mixed with Burnt Umber.

6. Paint lettering with Ivory Black. *Option: Use ink pen.*

Wooden Table:
1. Base with Burnt Umber.

2. With a liner brush, add criss cross strokes with Burnt Umber, Raw Sienna, and Raw Sienna mixed with Wicker White.

Red Birdhouse:
1. Base with Napthol Crimson. Shade with Napthol Crimson mixed with Ivory Black.

2. Paint lines and entrance holes with Ivory Black. Highlight with Wicker White.

3. Paint roof with Napthol Crimson mixed with Wicker White. Highlight Wicker White on base.

4. Base nest with Burnt Umber. Using a liner brush, add criss cross strokes with Burnt Umber, Raw Sienna, and Raw Sienna mixed with Wicker White.

Green Birdhouse:
1. Base walls with two coats Hunter Green. Shade with Hunter Green mixed with Ivory Black.

2. Paint entrance hole with Ivory Black. On the left side,

make a half-moon highlight with Wicker White.

3. Paint linework with Ivory Black. Highlight with Wicker White.

4. Paint base with Ivory Black. Highlight with Wicker White.

5. Paint checks on roof and outline with Ivory Black.

6. Paint pole with Burnt Umber.

7. Base ribbon with Yellow Medium. Shade with Burnt Sienna. Highlight with Wicker White.

Clay Pot:
1. Base with Burnt Sienna. Shade with Burnt Umber under rim, on sides, and on bottom. Along center add tints of Red Light.

2. Highlight and trim around top with Yellow Medium mixed with Wicker White.

Crock:
1. Paint top half with Burnt Umber. Shade with Ivory Black under rim.

2. Dry-brush tip of rim and sides with Raw Sienna. Highlight center of crock with Raw Sienna mixed with Wicker White.

3. Paint "#15" on bottom half of pot with Burnt Umber. From the outer edges, pull inward with Raw Sienna and Raw Sienna mixed with Burnt Umber.

4. Shade behind apples with Burnt Umber. Add a tint of Red Light to reflect apple color.

Apples:
1. Base apples with Red Light. Let dry.

2. Rewet each apple with Red Light. Shade with Red Light mixed with Ivory Black, using photo as a guide for placement. If needed, add more Red Light to separate apples. Leave a reflected light area on front of each apple.

3. Highlight with Red Light mixed with Yellow Medium and Yellow Medium mixed with Wicker White.

4. Paint stems Ivory Black. Highlight with Wicker White.

Bowl:
Wicker White is the base color of the bowl.

1. Shade with Ivory Black mixed with Wicker White. Make certain center is light; add more Wicker White as needed.

2. Add a line of Red Light around rim.

3. Paint chipped areas Ivory Black. Highlight on top with Wicker White. Add rusty areas with washes of Burnt Sienna.

Sunflower Bouquet:
1. Base sunflower petals with Burnt Sienna. Overstroke with Yellow Medium and Yellow Medium mixed with Wicker White. Using a liner, separate petals with Burnt Sienna.

2. Paint centers with Burnt Umber. Dab highlights with Yellow Medium mixed with Wicker White.

Continued on page 37

Still Life Lap Desk Pattern

Pattern is actual size

Continued from page 35

3. Paint stems with Burnt Umber. Paint leaves with Hunter Green. Highlight with Hunter Green mixed with Yellow Medium. Paint vein lines with Ivory Black.

4. Base cranberries with Red Light. Shade with Red Light mixed with Burnt Umber. Highlight with Red Light mixed with Wicker White. Add dots of Wicker White. Paint blossom ends with Ivory Black. Paint stems with Burnt Umber. Let dry.

FINISH

1. Apply waterbase varnish. Let dry.

2. Reassemble lap desk.

Birdhouses Country Crock

Pictured on page 38

Designed by
Faith Rollins

A great bowl to fill with apples or nuts. Cutting a stencil for each birdhouse shape makes basecoating quick and easy. See the Birdhouse Worksheet on page 39 for instructions.

GATHER THESE SUPPLIES

Painting Surface:
Ceramic crock with blue
stripes and glazed
finish (oven-proof) 6" x 9½"

Paints, Stains, and Finishes:
Acrylic gloss enamel paints:
Arbor Green

Black
Coffee Bean
Eggshell
Real Red
Spice Tan
Tangerine
Teal

Brushes:
Flat brushes
Liner
Old toothbrush
Round brushes
Script liners
Stencil brush

Other Supplies:
Craft knife
Masking tape
Stencil blank material

INSTRUCTIONS

Prepare:
1. Wipe crock with a damp cloth. Let dry.

2. Use Birdhouse Worksheet on page 39 to cut birdhouse stencils. Make a separate stencil for each birdhouse, the perch, and each roof.

3. Measure around the crock and divide into equal sections, spacing birdhouses around it. Mark placement, using photo as a guide.

PAINT THE DESIGN

Birdhouse #1:
1. Stencil house with Teal. Let dry. Apply a second coat.

2. Stencil upper section with Arbor Green. Stencil roof and entrance hole with Black.

3. Shade on upper section with a float of Arbor Green mixed with Black.

4. Paint board lines with thinned Arbor Green mixed with Black. Shade on lower section and inside the entrance hole with a mix of Teal mixed with Black.

Birdhouse #2:
1. Stencil house with Eggshell. Let dry. Apply a second coat.

2. Stencil roof with Real Red mixed with Coffee Bean and Tangerine. Stencil entrance hole and perch with Black.

3. Shade house with a float of Spice Tan. Shade inside entrance hole and highlight perch with thinned Eggshell.

Birdhouse #3:
1. Stencil house with red mix used on roof of birdhouse #2. Let dry. Apply a second coat.

2. Stencil roof with Arbor Green. Stencil entrance holes and perches with Black.

3. Shade inside entrance hole with thinned red mix. Shade on house and paint board lines with red mix mixed with Black.

4. Add wood grain lines with thinned shading color.

FINISH

1. Flyspeck crock with Black. Let dry for at least 24 hours.

2. Place crock in oven and bake for 10 minutes at 350°.

Note: Painted surface should not come in contact with foods. Clean with damp cloth.

Birdhouses Country Crock
Instructions begin on page 37

Birdhouse Worksheet

1. Stencil entire house.

2. Stencil eaves, roof, entrance hole, and perch.

3. Shade on eaves and lower section. Paint board lines.

4. Shade inside entrance hole.

Entrance Holes:
Use a circle template for ease in painting entrance holes. Use template as a stencil. After stenciling the hole, slide template slightly to the right. Draw a line on left side of template. Paint with shading color. Always paint perch in the direction of the shading inside the hole.

Birdhouse Crock Patterns

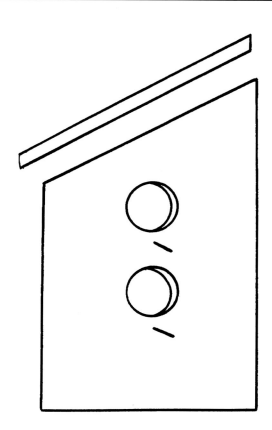

Patterns are actual size

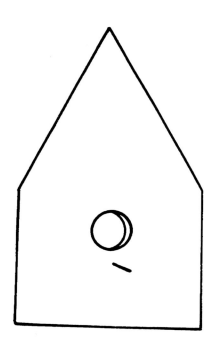

Sunflower Birdhouse

Instructions begin on page 42

Sunflower Birdhouse

Pictured on page 41

Designed by
Faith Rollins

This gourd-shaped bird-house has a curved, slatted roof and is easy to make.

GATHER THESE SUPPLIES

Painting Surface:
Gourd-shaped birdhouse,
  5¼" x 5¼" x 5":
  Front & back:
    cut from ¾" pine
  Top: 1¾" x 5",
    cut from ¼" pine
  Bottom: 3" x 3¾",
    cut from ⅛" Baltic birch
  Sides: 17 slats, ¼" x ¾" x 5"
  Perch: ¼" x 1¼" dowel

Paints, Stains, and Finishes:
Acrylic craft paints:
  Acorn Brown
  Burnt Umber
  Indigo
  Licorice
  Nutmeg
  Olive Green
  Raw Umber
  School Bus Yellow
  Sunflower
  Tapioca
  Yellow Ochre
Antiquing medium:
  Down Home Brown
Matte spray sealer

Brushes:
Flat brushes
Liner
Old toothbrush
Round brushes
Script liners

Other Supplies:
Drill & drill bits
Hammer
Hot glue gun & glue sticks
Sandpaper
Small nails
Tack cloth
Wood glue
Spanish moss

INSTRUCTIONS

Assemble and Base-coat:
1. Cut pieces as directed using Sunflower Birdhouse Front and Back Patterns on pages 44 and 45. Drill holes in front piece as shown on pattern.

2. Assemble birdhouse by gluing and nailing front and back pieces of house to bottom. Cut one slat in half and use halves to start sides of house. Nail slats to sides of house moving from bottom up and then add top piece.

3. Paint front and back with Tapioca.

4. Paint roof and side pieces with a wash of Burnt Umber.

5. Paint perch with Licorice.

6. Sand all areas and wipe with tack cloth.

7. Apply a second coat of Tapioca to front and back.

8. Paint roof and sides Indigo, allowing some Burnt Umber to show through.

9. Float Olive Green mixed with Burnt Umber around the edges.

10. Transfer details on Sunflower Birdhouse Front and Back Patterns on pages 44 and 45 to birdhouse.

PAINT THE DESIGN

Sunflowers:
1. Paint petals on front of the birdhouse with a double load of Sunflower and School Bus Yellow. Shade with a float of Nutmeg.

2. Outline petals with Yellow Ochre.

3. Stipple centers Raw Umber.

4. Stipple shadow areas Burnt Umber.

5. Stipple highlight areas Nutmeg.

Leaves and Vines:
1. Paint 2-stroke leaves on both the front and the back of birdhouse with Olive Green.

2. Paint line work, stems, and vines Olive Green.

3. Outline leaves with Olive Green.

Crow's Perch:
1. Paint board under crow on front of birdhouse with Raw Umber.

2. Shade with Burnt Umber. Highlight with Acorn Brown.

Crow:
1. Paint crow on both front and back of the birdhouse with Licorice.

2. Highlight crow's wing, head, and chest by floating with Licorice mixed with Tapioca.

3. Paint crow's eye with a dot of Yellow Ochre. When dry, add a small Licorice pupil on top of the Yellow Ochre dot.

FINISH

1. Flyspeck design with Licorice.

2. Lightly spray with matte spray sealer. Let dry.

3. Antique with Down Home Brown, wiping off excess. Let dry.

4. Very lightly spray entire house with matte spray sealer. Let dry.

5. Hot-glue Spanish moss in entrance hole.

6. Push perch in drilled hole.

Springtime Wildflowers Cabinet

Pictured on page 46

Designed by
Faith Rollins

This rustic wooden cabinet was designed to hold spare rolls of tissue in the bathroom. Use this charming pattern on any tall thin furniture piece. If the pattern is too tall, shorten by decreasing the length of the birdhouse pole.

GATHER THESE SUPPLIES

Painting Surface:
Wooden tissue cabinet or
other furniture piece

Paints, Stains, and Finishes:
Acrylic craft paints:
  Burnt Umber
  Country Twill
  Huckleberry
  Indigo
  Licorice
  Nutmeg
  Raw Sienna
  Slate Blue
  Sunflower
  Tapioca
  Teal Green
  Wrought Iron
  Yellow Ochre
Acrylic painting medium:
  extender
Oil paint:
  Burnt Umber
Matte spray sealer

Brushes:
Flat brushes
Liner
Old toothbrush
Round brushes
Script liners

Other Supplies:
Sandpaper
Small nails
Tack cloth
Wood glue

INSTRUCTIONS

Prepare and Base-coat:
1. Prepare wood. See Surface Preparation on page 7.

2. Paint cabinet, knob, and closure tab with Slate Blue mixed with Teal.

3. Sand cabinet, sanding heavier around edges to remove some paint for a worn look. Sand knob and closure tab. Wipe with a tack cloth.

4. Paint door of cabinet with two coats of Tapioca.

5. Transfer Springtime Wildflowers Cabinet Pattern on page 48 to the door.

PAINT THE DESIGN

Fence:
1. Paint fence with Country Twill.

2. Shade with Burnt Umber.

Birdhouse:
1. Paint pole with Raw Sienna. Shade with Burnt Umber.

2. Paint birdhouse Slate Blue mixed with Teal. Shade with Indigo.

3. Paint roof and base with Huckleberry. Highlight with Huckleberry mixed with Tapioca.

4. Paint entrance holes and perches with Licorice.

5. Shade under perches with Indigo.

6. Highlight perches with Licorice mixed with Tapioca.

7. Shade inside entrance holes with thinned Slate Blue mixed with Teal and Licorice.

8. Paint vertical lines on the side of the birdhouse to look like boards and indicate a crackled effect on the center birdhouse with thinned Indigo.

Greenery and Flowers:
1. Paint grass, weeds, and vine with Wrought Iron.

Sunflower Birdhouse Front Pattern

Pattern is actual size

Sunflower Birdhouse Back Pattern

Pattern is actual size

Continued from page 43

2. Dab Wrought Iron on some of the weeds to indicate leaves.

3. Paint leaves on vine with Wrought Iron.

4. Paint flowers with a double load of Yellow Ochre and Sunflower.

5. Dab flower centers with Huckleberry.

6. Add a highlight to flower centers with Huckleberry mixed with Tapioca.

7. Shade next to centers on petals with Nutmeg.

Birds:
1. Paint flying birds with Licorice.

FINISH

1. Spatter cabinet door with Licorice.

2. Lightly spray with matte spray sealer.

3. Antique with Burnt Umber oil paint and extender, wiping out highlights and darkening along edges.

4. Thin Burnt Umber paint with acrylic painting medium. Stain inside of cabinet.

5. Rub Burnt Umber oil paint on all metal pieces to antique.

Birdhouses & Wildflowers French Buckets

Pictured on page 49

Designed by
Donna Dewberry

These French buckets are wonderful for holding flowers or umbrellas. The Leaves Worksheet on page 51 and Wildflower Worksheet on page 52 illustrate the painting techniques used.

Large French Bucket

GATHER THESE SUPPLIES

Painting Surface:
French bucket,
   7" diameter, 12" tall

Paints, Stains, and Finishes:
Acrylic craft paints:
   Antique White
   Black
   Burnt Umber
   Green Forest
   Prussian Blue
   Tapestry Wine
   Wicker White
Matte spray sealer

Brushes:
Flat brushes
Script liner

INSTRUCTIONS

Prepare:
1. Prepare bucket. See Surface Preparation on page 7.

2. Transfer Large Birdhouse French Bucket Pattern on page 53 to large bucket.

PAINT THE DESIGN

Birdhouse:
1. Base-coat with Antique White. Let dry.

2. Load flat brush with Prussian Blue. Paint each side of roof in one continuous stroke. Let dry.

3. Double-load flat brush with Burnt Umber and Antique White. Paint vertical strokes on birdhouse to look like siding.

4. Load flat brush with Burnt Umber. Pick up Black on edge of brush. Paint a circle for entrance hole with Black on outer edge. Using chisel edge of same brush with same paint, paint a line ¼" wide for perch. Form a small circle at the end.

5. Load flat brush with Burnt Umber. Paint four short vertical strokes for base.

Branches:
1. Load flat brush with Burnt Umber. Paint branches and berry stems above birdhouse using chisel edge. Let dry.

Leaves:
1. Paint leaves, using one-stroke technique. See Leaves Worksheet on page 51.

2. Use chisel edge of brush to paint green stems on leaves across front of birdhouse.

Berries:
1. Dip handle end of brush in Tapestry Wine. Dot on bucket to make berries.

Springtime Wildflowers Cabinet Pattern

Birdhouse Hanger:
1. Load script liner with Black and paint loop over branch with tip of brush. Let dry.

FINISH

1. Spray with two coats of matte spray sealer.

Small French Bucket

GATHER THESE SUPPLIES

Painting Surface:
French bucket,
    5" diameter, 8" tall

Paints, Stains, and Finishes:
Acrylic craft paints:
    Black
    Dioxazine Purple
    Green Forest
    Napthol Crimson
    Prussian Blue
    White
    Yellow
Metallic acrylic craft paints:
    Rose Shimmer
Matte spray sealer

Brushes:
Flat brushes
Script liner

INSTRUCTIONS

Prepare:
1. Prepare bucket. See Surface Preparation on page 7.

2. Transfer Small Birdhouse French Bucket Pattern on page 54 onto small bucket.
Continued on page 50

Birdhouses & Wildflowers
French Buckets
Instructions begin
on page 47

Continued from page 48

PAINT THE DESIGN

Birdhouse:
1. Load flat brush with White. Using chisel edge of brush, paint post. Reload brush and paint walls of house. Let dry.

2. Load flat brush with Prussian Blue. Paint roof and base.

3. Load flat brush with Black. Paint a dot for entrance.

4. Load script liner with Black. Paint perch. Let dry.

Grass:
1. Paint grass. See Wildflowers Worksheet on page 52.

Red Flowers:
1. Double-load flat brush with Napthol Crimson and White. Paint C-strokes, working from top to bottom, with Napthol Crimson toward top of flower. See single C-stroke flowers on Wildflowers Worksheet on page 52.

Blue Flowers:
1. Load same brush with Prussian Blue and White. Paint blue flowers, making C-strokes with Prussian Blue towards top.

Yellow Flowers:
1. Double-load brush with Yellow and White. Paint C-stroke flowers placing Yellow at outer edge. See five stroke flowers on Wildflowers Worksheet on page 52. Dot flower centers with Napthol Crimson.

Purple Flowers:
1. Double-load flat brush with Dioxazine Purple and White. Stipple along blades of grass from top to bottom. See stippled flowers on Wildflowers Worksheet on page 52.

FINISH

1. Spray with two coats of matte spray sealer.

Time to Quilt Townhouse

Pictured on page 55

Designed by
Delores Lennon

This clock in a birdhouse is for bird, flower, and quilt lovers everywhere.

GATHER THESE SUPPLIES

Painting Surface:
Wooden Victorian
    clock birdhouse

Paints, Stains, and Finishes:
Acrylic craft paints:
    Alizarin Crimson
    Aspen Green
    Berries 'n Cream
    Dioxazine Purple
    Ivory Black
    Linen
    Maroon
    Raspberry Sherbet
    Raw Sienna
    Raw Umber
    Southern Pine
    Taffy
    Titanium White
    Ultramarine Blue
    Warm White
    Wicker White
    Yellow Light
    Yellow Ochre

Acrylic painting medium:
    extender
Waterbase varnish
Matte spray sealer

Brushes:
Flat brushes
Liner
Round brush

Other Supplies:
Masking tape
Permanent black ink pen
Small amount of moss or
    small twigs
Small bird
White craft glue

INSTRUCTIONS

Prepare and Base-coat:
1. Disassemble birdhouse. Remove clock works.

2. Prepare wood. See Surface Preparation on page 7.

3. Paint entire birdhouse with two coats of Linen. Let dry between coats.

4. Paint Victorian woodwork with Wicker White. Paint base of house with Southern Pine.

5. Transfer pattern lines to roof tops and front of house. Do not transfer details on roof tops.

PAINT THE DESIGN

Roof Tops:
Before painting, tape around each section. When dry, remove tape and retape another section. Then paint that section. This eliminates the need for perfect hand control and will give excellent lines.

Continued on page 53

Leaves Worksheet

Fill in leaf shape with "S" strokes, having dark edge of brush towards outside of leaf.

Add curlicue tendrils with inky Green Forest. supporting the hand with the pinky finger.

Ivy Leaves

One Stroke Leaves

Push, turn, and lift with brush.

Double-load a flat brush with White and Green Forest.

Broad Leaves with Lacy Edges

Double-load a flat brush with White and Green Forest.

Turned Edge Leaves

Double-load flat brush with White and Green Forest.

Stroke with Green Forest on outer edge. Turn brush on chisel edge.

Fill in leaf shape with Green Forest on outside. Wiggle brush on outer edge to shape leaf.

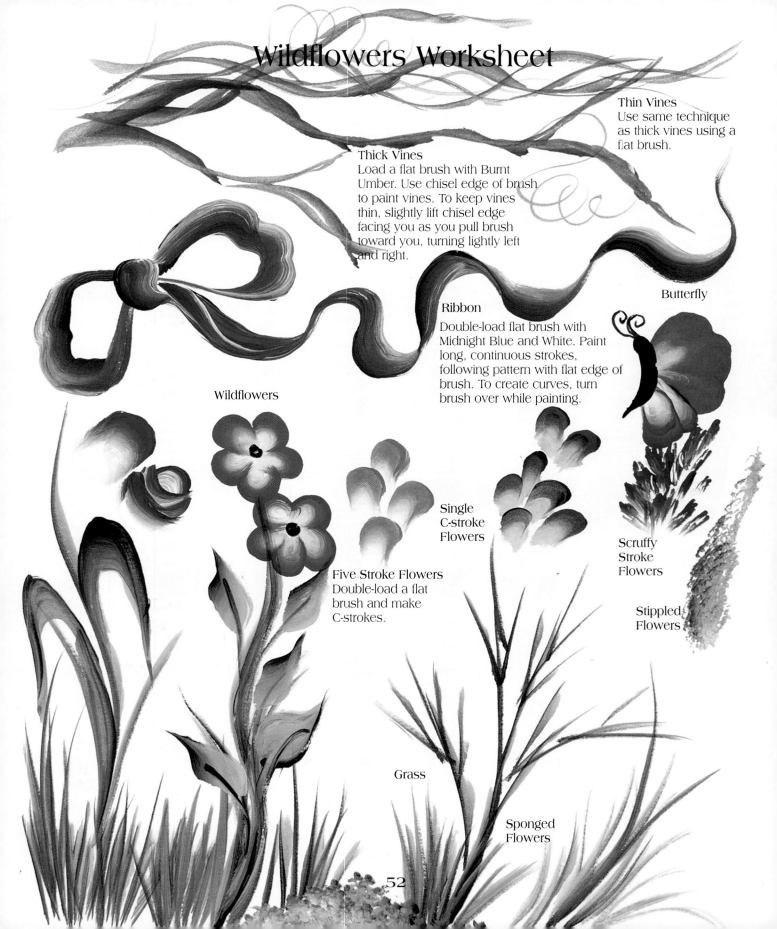

Wildflowers Worksheet

Thin Vines
Use same technique as thick vines using a flat brush.

Thick Vines
Load a flat brush with Burnt Umber. Use chisel edge of brush to paint vines. To keep vines thin, slightly lift chisel edge facing you as you pull brush toward you, turning lightly left and right.

Butterfly

Ribbon
Double-load flat brush with Midnight Blue and White. Paint long, continuous strokes, following pattern with flat edge of brush. To create curves, turn brush over while painting.

Wildflowers

Single C-stroke Flowers

Scruffy Stroke Flowers

Five Stroke Flowers
Double-load a flat brush and make C-strokes.

Stippled Flowers

Grass

Sponged Flowers

52

Continued from page 50

Base each section with two coats of color indicated.

1. Paint green section with Southern Pine.

2. Paint pink sections with Berries 'n Cream.

3. Paint red sections with Maroon.

4. Paint cream sections with Taffy.

5. When each section is dry, transfer pattern lines, using Time to Quilt Townhouse Roof and Bird Hole Patterns on pages 56 and 57. (There are no lines on green sections.)

6. Paint flowers on pink sections with thin dots of Maroon. Paint leaves with thinned Aspen Green.

7. Paint squiggles on red sections with thinned Raspberry Sherbet.

8. Paint dots on cream sections with Southern Pine.

9. Paint lace trim with two coats Warm White.

Paint Mixes:
Mix the following colors on a waxed palette and store on a damp paper towel.

Roses Mix:
#1 Medium is Titanium White mixed with Alizarin Crimson, Dioxazine Purple, and Raw Umber.
#2 Dark is mostly Raw Umber mixed with Alizarin Crimson.
#3 Light is medium #1 mixed

with lots of Titanium White and a touch of Yellow Light.

Leaves Mix:
#1 Medium is Ivory Black mixed with Yellow Light and a touch of Titanium White.
#2 Dark is medium #1 mixed with Ivory Black.
#3 Light is medium #1 mixed with more Titanium White and

a touch of Yellow Light. Add a touch of Ultramarine Blue to the three leaf mixes separately for blue-green mixes.

Roses:
1. Apply dark mix to shadow areas, light mix to light areas.
Continued on page 56

Large Birdhouses
French Bucket Pattern

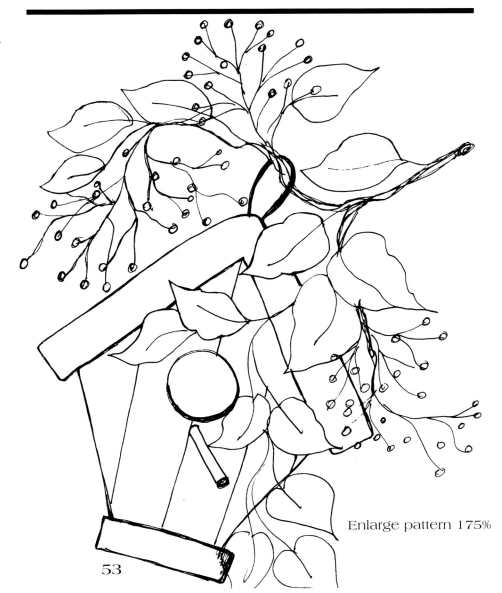

Enlarge pattern 175%

Small Birdhouse
French Bucket Pattern

Pattern is actual size

Continued from page 53

Fill in rest of petals with medium mix. Blend between light and medium values first. Rinse brush. Blend between medium and dark areas.

2. Highlight some light areas with a touch of Titanium White. Paint gently into light areas.

Leaves:
1. Place dark mix in shadow areas. Place light mix on each side of center vein and along any edge which overlaps another leaf.

2. Fill in remaining area with medium mix. Blend as you did the roses.

3. Paint tendrils with thinned medium value mix using a liner.

Flower Centers:
1. Tap in a small amount of Yellow Ochre, filling in center.

2. Place a tiny amount of Raw Sienna along base of center. Tap in a tiny bit of Yellow Light on top of center.

3. Make dots around center with thinned Raw Sienna, then with thinned Yellow Light.

FINISH

1. When paint is thoroughly dry, fill in details with black ink pen. Lightly spray inking with matte spray sealer. Let dry.

2. Apply waterbase varnish. Let dry.

3. Reassemble clock and replace batteries. Reassemble birdhouse, using white craft glue, assembling one section at a time for better adhesion. Glue on Victorian woodwork.

4. Place bird with moss or twigs on front perch.

Church Birdhouse

Pictured on page 58

Designed by
Faith Rollins

This simple country church has a painted faux verdigris finish on its metal roof. You can make the birdhouse yourself from the patterns supplied.
Continued on page 59

Time to Quilt Townhouse Roof Patterns

Top

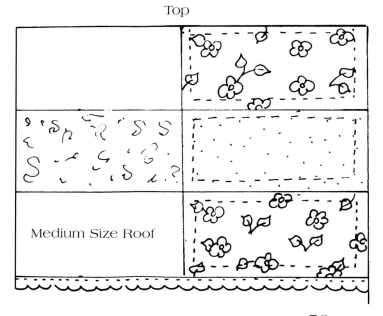

Medium Size Roof

Top

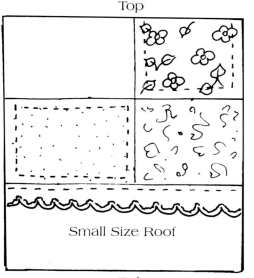

Small Size Roof

Enlarge pattern 130%

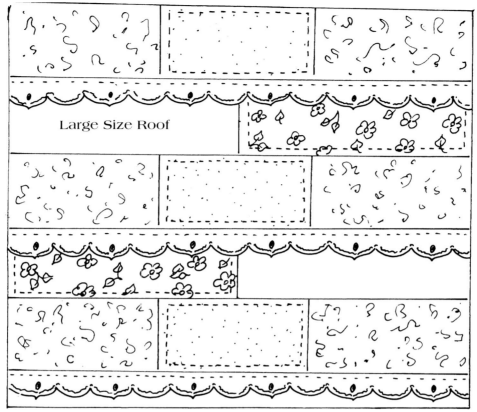

Large Size Roof

Enlarge pattern 125%

Time to Quilt Townhouse
Bird Hole Pattern

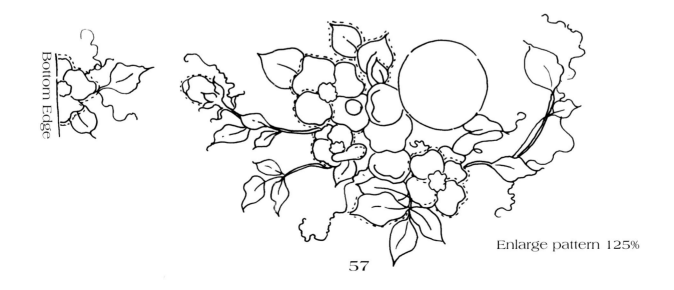

Bottom Edge

Enlarge pattern 125%

Church Birdhouse
Instructions begin on page 56

GATHER THESE SUPPLIES

Painting Surface:
Wooden church birdhouse:
    Front, back, and entrance
        cut from ¾" wood
    Sides and bottom
        cut from ¼" wood
    Steeple cut from 1½" wood
    ¼" wood dowel,
        1¼" long (for perch)
    Tin sheeting for roof

Paints, Stains, and Finishes:
Acrylic craft paints:
    Licorice
    Patina
    Tapioca
Metallic acrylic craft paints:
    Antique Copper
    Solid Bronze
Antiquing medium:
    Down Home Brown
Metal primer

Brushes:
Flat brushes
Liner
Old toothbrush
Script liner
Sponge brush

Other Supplies:
Craft knife
Drill
Finishing nails
Hammer
Sandpaper
Saw
Sea sponge
Spanish moss
Tin snips
Wood glue

Optional: Stencil blank material

INSTRUCTIONS

Prepare and Base-coat:
1. Prepare wood. See Surface Preparation on page 7.

2. Transfer Church Birdhouse Patterns on pages 60 and 61 to wood. Cut out wood pieces.

3. Assemble front, back, sides, and bottom, using wood glue and finishing nails, to make main part of birdhouse.

4. Drill entrance hole and hole for perch.

5. Paint main part of birdhouse, entrance, and steeple with Tapioca. Let dry.

6. Sand wood pieces, removing paint from edges.

7. Transfer patterns for door and windows from the Church Birdhouse Patterns on pages 60 and 61.

Option: Cut stencils for door and windows.

Roof:
1. Cut tin for roof, allowing a ¼" overhang on all sides. On front, remember to allow ¼" beyond entrance piece.

2. Spray tin with metal primer. Let dry.

PAINT THE DESIGN

Door, Windows, Perch, and Cross:
1. Paint or stencil door and windows with Licorice.

2. Paint cross with Licorice.

3. Lightly sand these areas.

4. Outline door and windows with Patina.

5. Paint perch with Licorice.

Roof:
1. Paint roof with Patina. Let dry.

2. Sponge over Patina with Solid Bronze, but do not cover all of the Patina. Let dry.

3. Sponge with Antique Copper, overlapping other colors, but still leaving some Patina showing. Let dry.

FINISH

Spatter and Antique:
1. Spatter wood pieces with Licorice. Let dry.

2. Spray with matte spray sealer.

3. Antique with Down Home Brown. Let dry.

4. Spray again with matte spray sealer.

Assemble:
1. Glue entrance piece to front of church.

2. Glue or nail roof in place. If nailing, touch up nail heads with paint to match roof colors.

3. Attach steeple with glue.

4. Glue perch in pre-drilled hole.

5. Glue Spanish moss in entrance hole.

Church Birdhouse Patterns

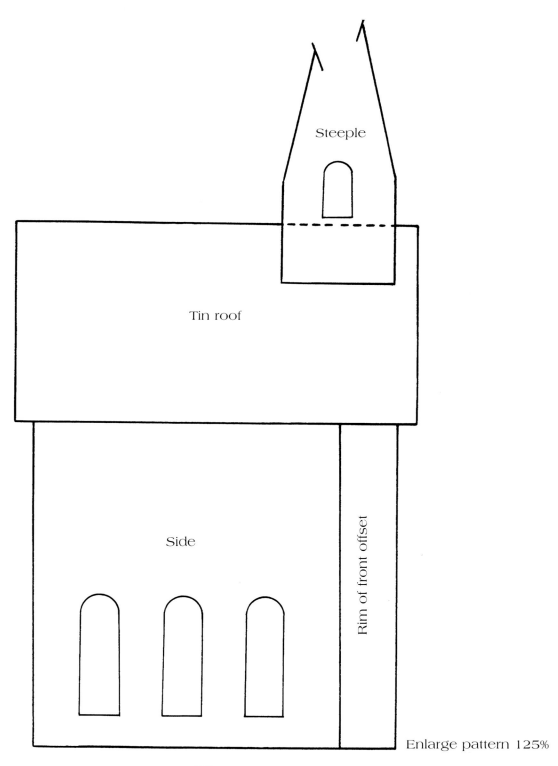

Steeple

Tin roof

Side

Rim of front offset

Enlarge pattern 125%

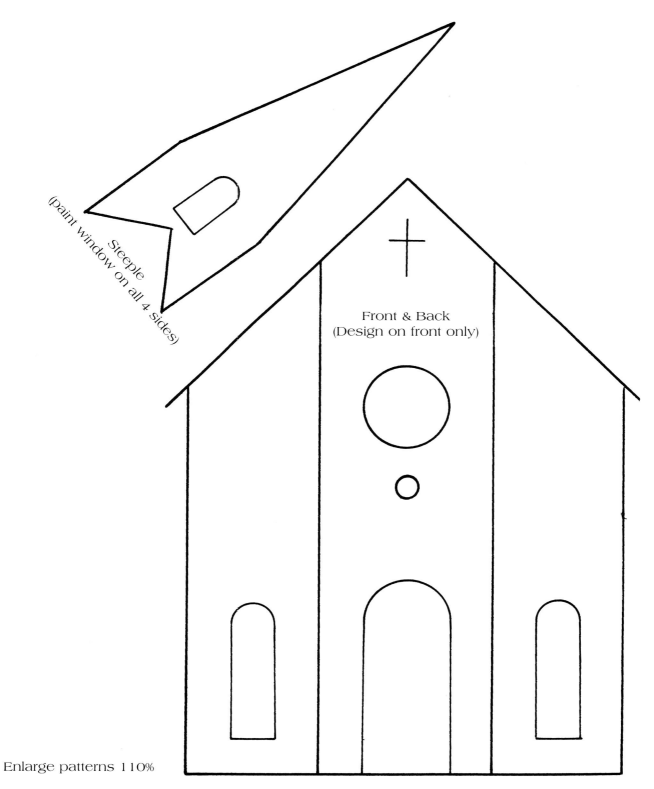

Steeple
(paint window on all 4 sides)

Front & Back
(Design on front only)

Enlarge patterns 110%

61

Santa & His Birdhouse

Pictured on page 62

Designed by
Faith Rollins

A birdhouse and holiday greenery decorate this Santa's staff. Make him yourself with the patterns provided.

GATHER THESE SUPPLIES

Painting Surface:
Wooden Santa with
　separate arms:
　Santa and arms
　　cut from ¾" wood
　Band on hat
　　cut from ½" wood
　Base cut from ¾"
　　weathered cedar
Wooden birdhouse:
　Front and back
　　cut from ¾"
　　weathered cedar
　Bottom, sides, and roof
　　cut from ⅜"
　　weathered cedar
Wooden dowel,
　⅜" diameter, 1⅜" long
　(for attaching arms)
Wooden dowel,
　⅜" diameter, 35" long
　(for birdhouse post)

Paints, Stains, and Finishes:
Acrylic craft paints:
　Barn Wood
　Barnyard Red
　Bluebonnet
　Calico Red
　Cinnamon
　Licorice
　Light Red Oxide
　Medium Gray
　Portrait
　Tapioca
　Wicker White

Antiquing medium:
　Down Home Brown
Matte spray sealer

Brushes:
Deerfoot brush
Flat brushes
Liner
Round brushes
Script liners
Sponge brushes

Other Supplies:
Twig bow: 10" wide
Greenery and dried flowers,
　small cones, berries
Spanish moss
Christmas ribbon:
　red/green plaid, 1 yd.
Drill & drill bits
Finishing nails
Floral wire
Hot glue gun & glue sticks
Sandpaper
Saw
Wood glue
Wood screws

INSTRUCTIONS

Prepare and Base-coat:
1. Prepare wood. See Surface Preparation on page 7.

2. Transfer Santa & His Birdhouse Patterns on pages 64 and 65 to wood. Cut out wood pieces.

3. Drill holes in one hand and base of body for post.

4. Paint Santa pieces except base with Tapioca. Let dry.

5. Sand, removing some paint from edges. Wipe away dust.

6. Transfer hair and beard pattern lines from Santa & His Birdhouse Patterns on page 65.

Base-coat Santa:
1. Paint coat, hat, and sleeves with Barnyard Red mixed with Calico Red.

2. Paint gloves with Licorice.

3. Paint face with Portrait. Let dry. Sand again. Apply a second coat to these areas. Let dry.

4. Shade between coat and hat with a float of Barnyard Red mixed with Licorice. Let dry.

5. Transfer facial features and mustache from Santa & His Birdhouse Patterns on page 65.

Prepare Birdhouse:
1. Assemble birdhouse with finishing nails.

2. Drill hole in bottom for dowel and in front for entrance hole.

PAINT THE DESIGN

Face and Eye:
1. Shade around face with Cinnamon.

2. Paint eye area with Wicker White.

3. Shade around eyebrow and above and below eye with Cinnamon, pulling out wrinkle lines. Let dry.

4. Paint pupil with Licorice. Paint iris with Bluebonnet.

5. Shade eye with Medium Gray. Highlight pupil and iris with Wicker White.

6. Outline eye with Cinnamon.

7. Paint eyelashes with Licorice.

8. Add a bright highlight of Wicker White to pupil.

9. Float cheek area with Light Red Oxide mixed with Wicker White. Let dry and repeat to intensify.

Hair and Fur:
1. Wash eyebrow, hair, beard, mustache, and fur with Medium Gray.

2. Add strokes with a liner double-loaded with Tapioca and Barn Wood. Highlight with strokes of Wicker White.

3. Stipple fur with a deerfoot brush double-loaded with Tapioca and Barn Wood.

4. Stipple fur with Wicker White to highlight, but don't cover all of the shadow color. (If you get carried away with the lighter colors, stipple some dark color back in). Let dry.

FINISH

Santa:
1. Spray Santa pieces with matte spray sealer.

2. Antique with Down Home Brown. Let dry.

3. Spray again with matte spray sealer.

4. Attach arms with 1⅜" long dowel, drilling through body and into insides of arms.

5. Attach Santa to base with wood screws.

Decorate Birdhouse and Base:
1. Hot-glue birdhouse to top end of long dowel.

2. Make a multi-loop bow with Christmas ribbon.

3. Glue bow, greenery, and dried flowers to twig bow. See photo on page 62 as a guide.

4. Hot-glue twig bow to birdhouse post and hold in place until glue sets. Reinforce with wire. Cover wire with a piece of ribbon.

5. Hot-glue Spanish moss to base, roof of birdhouse, and in entrance hole.

6. Hot-glue ribbon, greenery, and dried flowers to Santa's base and roof of birdhouse.

7. Push post through drilled hole in Santa's hand and the drilled hole in base.

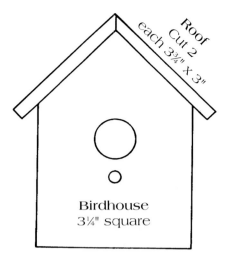

Birdhouse
3¼" square

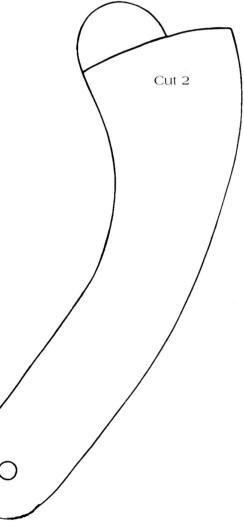

Cut 2

Santa & His Birdhouse Patterns

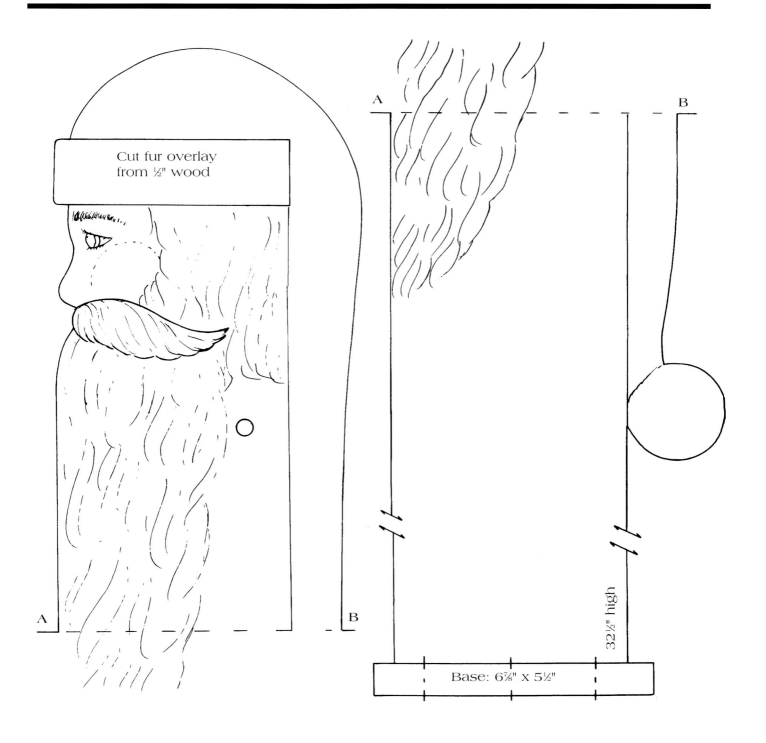

Cut fur overlay
from ½" wood

A

B

A

B

Base: 6⅞" x 5½"

32½" high

Checkerboard & Ivy Birdhouse & Bird Feeder

Pictured on page 66

Designed by
Sue Bailey

The red and white checks and green ivy leaves lend a coordinated theme to this wooden birdhouse and terra-cotta bird feeder made from a clay pot and saucer.

Birdhouse

GATHER THESE SUPPLIES

Painting Surface:
Birdhouse, 11" tall with
    copper on roof ridge

Paints, Stains, and Finishes:
Acrylic craft paints:
    Burnt Sienna
    Glazed Carrots
    Hunter Green
    Ivory Black
    Napthol Crimson
    Raw Sienna
    Tapioca
    Titanium White
    True Blue
    Yellow Medium
Waterbase varnish
Gloss spray sealer

Brushes:
Flat brushes
Liner
Sponge brushes

Other Supplies:
Masking tape, 1" wide
Sandpaper: 220 grit
Tack cloth

Optional: Polyurethane

INSTRUCTIONS

Prepare and Base-coat:
1. Prepare wood. See Surface Preparation on page 7.

2. Seal surface with water-base varnish.

3. Paint with Tapioca. Let dry.

4. Trace and transfer Checker-board & Ivy Birdhouse Pattern on page 68.

5. Using masking tape, create a checkerboard on left and right sides of birdhouse, placing strips of tape 1" wide 1" apart from top to bottom. Then place strips 1" apart, perpendicular to the first set of strips. Paint open spaces with Napthol Crimson. Let dry. Remove tape.

PAINT THE DESIGN

Window:
1. Paint window opening with Ivory Black.

2. Paint sash with Titanium White.

3. Base shutters with Napthol Crimson. Shade with Napthol Crimson mixed with Ivory Black. Highlight with Glazed Carrots.

4. Paint line work with Ivory Black. Let dry.

5. Paint a shadow in back of the shutters with a wash of Ivory Black.

Window Box:
1. Base-coat box with Raw Sienna, Raw Sienna mixed with Burnt Umber, and Raw Sienna mixed with Titanium White. Using a liner, add lines with Burnt Umber to look like wood grain.

2. Paint leaves and greenery with Ivory Black, Hunter Green, Yellow Medium, and Titanium White.

3. Paint stems with Hunter Green.

4. Using a flat brush, paint red geraniums by dabbing Napthol Crimson. Highlight with Glazed Carrots and Glazed Carrots mixed with Titanium White.

5. Paint blue flowers by dabbing with True Blue and True Blue mixed with Titanium White.

6. Paint white flowers by dabbing Titanium White.

7. Paint ivy leaves with Hunter Green. Highlight with Yellow Medium mixed with Titanium White. Outline leaves and paint vines with Ivory Black. Let dry.

FINISH

1. Spray with gloss sealer.

Note: If using outdoors, use polyurethane.

Bird Feeder

GATHER THESE SUPPLIES

Painting Surfaces:
Clay pot, 6"
Clay saucer, 8"

Checkerboard & Ivy Birdhouse Pattern

Paints, Stains, and Finishes:
Acrylic craft paints:
    Hunter Green
    Ivory Black
    Napthol Crimson
    Tapioca
    Titanium White
    Yellow Medium
Gloss spray sealer

Brushes:
Flat brushes
Liner
Sponge brushes

Other Supplies:
Drill and ⅜" masonry bit
Epoxy glue
Masking tape: 1" wide
Natural jute cord:
    4-ply (2 yds.)
Wooden wheels: ¾" diameter (4)

INSTRUCTIONS

Prepare and Base-coat:
1. Make certain pot and saucer are clean and dry. If not, wash and let dry.

2. Paint pot with Tapioca. Paint saucer and small wooden wheels with Napthol Crimson. Let dry.

3. Glue wheels inside saucer at 12 o'clock, 3 o'clock, 6 o'clock, and 9 o'clock. This will keep pot raised above saucer when pot is added, allowing bird feed to flow into saucer.

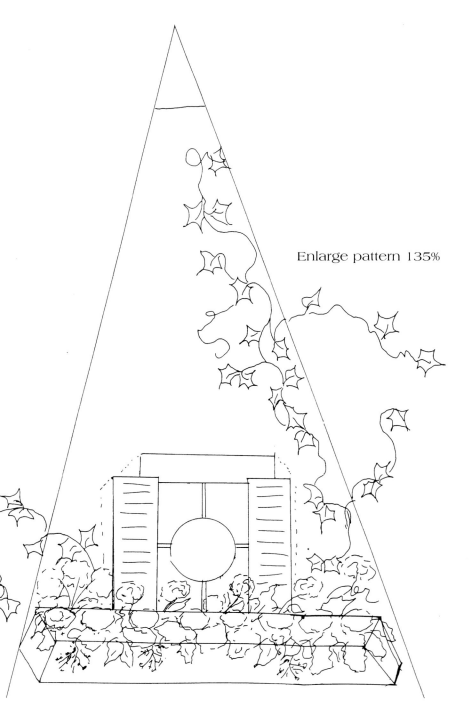

Enlarge pattern 135%

4. Using masking tape, create a checkerboard on rim of pot, placing strips of tape 1" wide 1" apart. Then place strips 1" apart, perpendicular to the first set of strips. Paint open spaces with Napthol Crimson. Let dry. Remove tape.

5. Transfer Checkerboard & Ivy Bird Feeder Pattern onto pot.

PAINT THE DESIGN

1. Base-coat ivy leaves with Hunter Green. Highlight with Yellow Medium mixed with Titanium White.

2. Outline leaves and paint vines with Ivory Black. Let dry.

3. Spray with gloss spray sealer. Let dry.

FINISH

1. Drill hole in bottom of saucer.

2. Fold jute cord in half. Pull folded end through hole in saucer and top of pot. Knot cord below saucer and at top of pot. To add bird seed, untie knot at top and fill pot.

Checkerboard & Ivy Bird Feeder Pattern

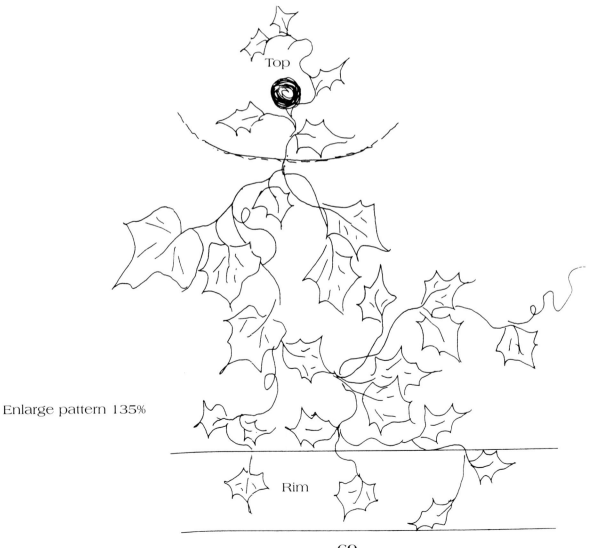

Enlarge pattern 135%

Bluebird Villa
Instructions begin on page 71

Bluebird Villa

Pictured on page 70

Designed by
Chris Stokes

Bluebirds like rustic houses that blend with surroundings. This one was made to mount on a tree.

GATHER THESE SUPPLIES

Painting Surface:
Wooden birdhouse, 17½" tall

Paints, Stains, and Finishes:
Acrylic craft paints:
    Alizarin Crimson
    Bayberry
    Berries 'n Cream
    Burnt Umber
    English Mustard
    Licorice
    Light Gray
    Midnight
    Tapioca
    Thicket
    Wicker White
    Yellow Light
Antiquing medium:
    Country Blue
Waterbase varnish

Brushes:
Fan brush
Flat brushes
Liner
Round brush
Stencil brush

Other Supplies:
Brown paper bags
Sandpaper: 220 grit
Tack cloth

INSTRUCTIONS

Prepare and Antique:
1. Prepare wood. See Surface Preparation on page 7.

2. Mix Country Blue antiquing medium with water and stain entire house, inside and out. Let dry. Sand with pieces of brown paper bag.

3. Transfer Bluebird Villa Patterns on pages 72-75 onto wooden birdhouse.

PAINT THE DESIGN

Fence:
1. Wash fence with Light Gray. Let dry.

Trees:
1. Stipple tree on front using a stencil brush double-loaded with Alizarin Crimson and Berries 'n Cream. Highlight with Tapioca.

2. Paint tree trunks on front and right sides using a flat brush double-loaded with Licorice and English Mustard. Highlight with Tapioca.

3. Stipple tree on right side using a stencil brush double-loaded with Thicket and Bayberry. Highlight with Tapioca.

Birdhouse, Pole, and Bench:
1. Paint birdhouse, pole, and bench with Tapioca. Shade with Burnt Umber.

2. Paint birdhouse roof with Bayberry. Highlight with Tapioca.

3. Paint hole with Licorice.

4. Paint cat with Tapioca. Shade with a small amount of Licorice. Paint cat's collar with Alizarin Crimson.

Flowers, Vines, and Greenery on Sides of House:
1. Stipple greenery around base of house with Thicket and Bayberry. Tap in flowers with mixes of Alizarin Crimson and Berries 'n Cream. Add more color with touches of Midnight.

2. Paint yellow flowers with Tapioca and a touch of Yellow Light. Paint centers with Burnt Umber. Pull up flower stems and leaves with inky Wicker White.

3. Paint vines on fence and left side with Thicket and Bayberry. Highlight with Tapioca. Paint roses on vines with mixes of Alizarin Crimson, Berries 'n Cream, and Tapioca.

4. Loosely pounce wisteria on left side with Midnight, Alizarin Crimson, and Tapioca.

Roof:
1. Rows of shingles are 1" apart. Using a fan brush, pull inky Licorice under each row. Then pull up highlights of inky Light Gray from bottom edges of rows.

2. Paint roof vines inky Licorice and English Mustard.

3. Paint leaves, double-loading brush with Bayberry and Thicket. Without washing brush, pick up Alizarin Crimson and Tapioca and Berries 'n Cream. Outline leaves with inky Wicker White.

4. Paint flowers with Wicker White and a touch of Yellow
Continued on page 77

Bluebird Villa Front Pattern

Pattern is actual size

Bluebird Villa Left Side Pattern

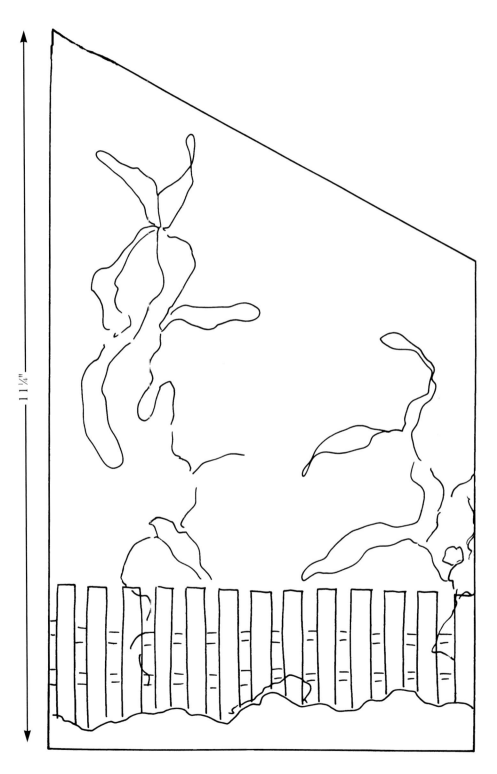

11 ¼"

Bluebird Villa Roof Pattern

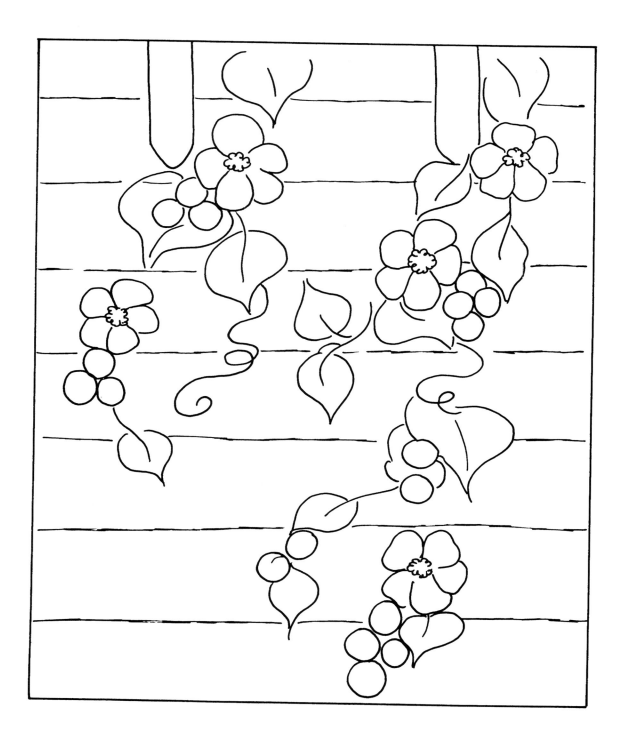

Pattern is actual size

Continue pattern onto back of house.

Bluebird Villa Right Side Pattern

11 ¼"

Sunflower
Birdhouse
Wall Plaque
Instructions
begin on
page 77

Continued from 71

Light. Pick up a bit of Alizarin Crimson on some. Shade petals lightly with Thicket. Paint highlight lines on petals with inky Tapioca, adding a touch of Alizarin Crimson to some. Paint centers with Thicket and highlight with dots of Tapioca.

5. To paint berries, double-load a flat brush with Alizarin Crimson and Tapioca and Alizarin Crimson and Berries 'n Cream in several values. Highlight with Wicker White.

6. Paint tendrils with inky greens and browns, mixing in touches of Wicker White and Alizarin Crimson. Let dry.

FINISH

1. Apply waterbase varnish. Let dry.

Sunflower Birdhouse Wall Plaque

Pictured on page 76

Designed by
Chris Stokes

GATHER THESE SUPPLIES

Painting Surface:
   9" x 24" framed wall
   plaque

Paints, Stains, and Finishes:
Acrylic craft paints:
   Barnyard Red
   Bayberry
   Burnt Sienna
   Burnt Umber

   English Mustard
   Licorice
   Sunflower
   Southern Pine
   Taffy
   True Blue
   Yellow Light
Antiquing medium:
   Down Home Brown
Crackle medium
Waterbase varnish

Brushes:
Flat brushes
Liner
Round brush
Sponge brush
Stencil brush

Other Supplies:
Blue bird: 4"
Artificial sunflowers:
   4" diameter with leaves (2)
Berry garland: 26" long
Brown paper bag
Jute rope: 30"
Natural sea sponge

INSTRUCTIONS

Prepare and Base-coat:
1. Prepare wood. See Surface Preparation on page 7.

2. Mix Down Home Brown antiquing medium with water and stain wood pieces. Let dry. Sand with pieces of brown paper bag.

3. Base-coat front of wall plaque with Sunflower. Let dry. Sand again. Using a natural sea sponge, sponge in sky area with True Blue and a touch of Taffy. When working downward, pick up more and more Taffy. Let dry.

4. Transfer Sunflower Birdhouse Wall Plaque Pattern on page 78.

PAINT THE DESIGN

Birdhouse:
1. Base-coat roof and house with English Mustard mixed with a touch of Sunflower. Let dry.

2. Paint roof with Barnyard Red. Use a "hit and miss" technique allowing the undercoat to show through.

3. Paint crackle medium on the house. Let dry thoroughly.

4. Paint over crackle medium with long vertical strokes of Taffy. Do not overlap strokes or overwork. Cracks will appear as Taffy dries.

5. Paint birdhouse entrance Licorice.

6. Paint rim of entrance double loaded Burnt Umber and Taffy.

7. Paint perch Taffy. Shade with Burnt Umber, then with Licorice. Highlight with Taffy.

8. Paint end of perch with Barnyard Red and highlight with Taffy.

Birdhouse Pole:
1. Base-coat with English Mustard. Shade with Burnt Umber. Re-shade with Licorice as needed. Let dry.

Vine Around Stake:
1. Transfer vine and sunflowers of Sunflower Birdhouse Wall Plaque Pattern on page 78.

2. Double-load liner brush with inky Burnt Umber and a touch of Southern Pine.

3. Wiggle in the vine.

4. Paint leaves with inky Southern Pine and inky True Blue double-loaded on a flat brush.

5. Paint berries Barnyard Red and Yellow Light double-loaded on a flat brush, then pick up True Blue on darkest corner of brush. Blend and layer berries in. Highlight berries with Taffy.

6. Paint tendrils with inky Burnt Umber.

Sunflowers:
1. Double-load stencil brush with Burnt Umber on outside and Burnt Sienna on inside. Stipple in flower centers.

2. For petals, double-load a round brush with Burnt Sienna and Yellow Light. Pull petals from center of flower outward, ending with a point. Let dry. Reload the same way with Taffy and Yellow Light and paint top petals.

Sunflower Leaves:
1. Wiggle in with double-loaded Sunflower and Southern Pine. Dab brush into Yellow Light now and then to give more color to leaves.

Frame:
1. Paint front surface only with Barnyard Red. Let dry.

2. Sand edges for an antique look.

Enlarge pattern 220%

1. Apply waterbase varnish. Let dry.

2. Tie a knot 5" from each end of jute rope and unravel ends up to knot. Staple rope just inside knots to top of frame on backside for hanger.

3. Staple berry garland to frame across top and upper left. Staple sunflowers at top left.

4. Wire blue bird to bottom of garland on left side.

Cottage Birdhouse Lamp

Pictured on page 81

Designed by
Chris Stokes

Light up a dark corner with this charming birdhouse lamp. The fabric lampshade is spattered with the colors used to paint the house.

GATHER THESE SUPPLIES

Painting Surface:
Wooden birdhouse, 13" tall

Paints, Stains, and Finishes:
Acrylic craft paints:
  Bayberry
  Berries 'n Cream
  Burnt Umber
  Emerald Isle
  Linen
  Midnight
  Raspberry Wine
  Warm White
Waterbase varnish

Brushes:
Flat brushes
Liner
Sponge brush
Stencil brush

Other Supplies:
Lamp shade: 12"
Lamp parts
  (socket, cord, and plug)
Sandpaper: 220 grit
Tack cloth

INSTRUCTIONS

Prepare and Base-coat:
1. Prepare wood. See Surface Preparation on page 7.

2. With sponge brush, base-coat roof with Raspberry Wine. Base-coat walls with Linen. Base-coat base with Emerald Isle.

3. Transfer Cottage Birdhouse Lamp Patterns on pages 80, 82-83.

PAINT THE DESIGN

Windows:
1. Paint window openings with Midnight. Paint shutters using flat brush double-loaded with Berries 'n Cream and Raspberry Wine.

2. Paint decorations at top with Warm White. In front window, paint bird cage with Warm White. Float in curtain with Warm White.

3. Float in window curtain on left side with Berries 'n Cream.

4. Pounce greenery in window boxes with stencil brush double-loaded with Emerald Isle and Bayberry.

Pounce in flowers with same brush double-loaded with Berries 'n Cream and Raspberry Wine.

Door:
1. Stain door with a wash of Burnt Umber.

2. Paint oval glass in door with Midnight. Paint etched design on glass with a small amount of Warm White.

3. Paint decorative line work with Linen. Shade door with Burnt Umber.

Chimney and Steps:
1. Base-coat chimney and steps in slip-slap fashion with Linen and Burnt Umber.

2. Paint lines with Midnight. Highlight with random floats of Warm White to form stones.

Flower Pots:
1. Paint with Warm White.

2. Shade with Burnt Umber.

Walls, Greenery, and Fence:
1. To paint half-timber wood trim, float Burnt Umber, using a flat brush.

2. Paint topiary trees around front door, vines on half-timber trim, and shrubbery around bottom of walls, double-loading with Bayberry and Emerald Isle.

3. Paint flowers, double-loading Raspberry Wine and Berries 'n Cream. Add vines with inky Burnt Umber.

4. Paint fence at back left corner with inky Warm White. Highlight with Warm White.

Details:

1. Spatter house with inky Raspberry Wine.

2. Paint curly line trim on edges of roof with Berries 'n Cream. Spatter roof with Berries 'n Cream. Let dry.

FINISH

1. Apply waterbase varnish. Let dry.

2. Spatter lampshade with all of the colors used on birdhouse.

3. Insert lamp socket at top of chimney. Connect wire. Insert light bulb and place shade on bulb.

Cottage Birdhouse Lamp Side Pattern

Enlarge pattern 145%

Cottage Birdhouse Lamp Top Pattern

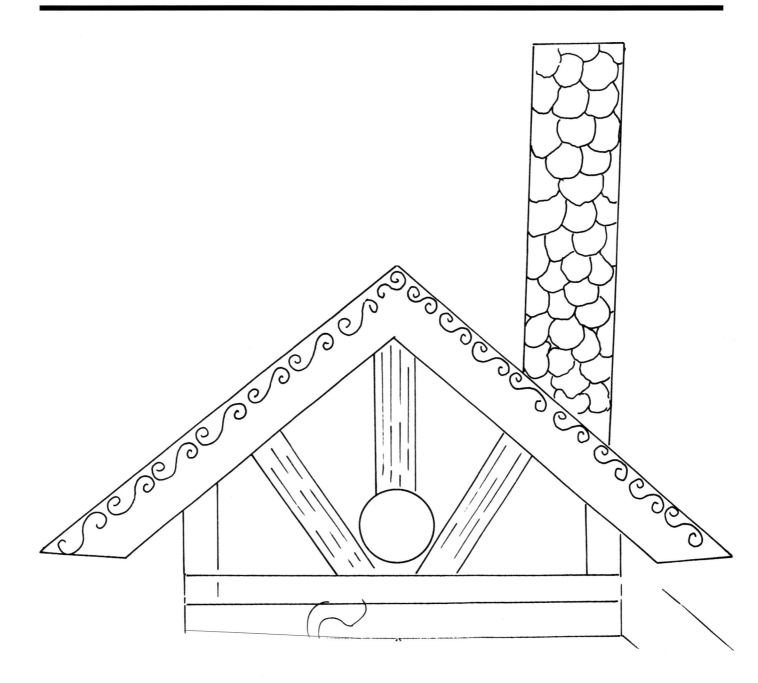

Enlarge pattern 125%

Cottage Birdhouse Lamp Bottom Pattern

Enlarge pattern 145%

Instructions begin on page 85

Bird's Eye View Lamp

Pictured on page 84

Designed by
Pat Wakefield

Baby birds in their nest adorn the shade of this birdhouse lamp. Daisies, iris, and hollyhocks grow around the picket fence on the birdhouse lamp base. The Bird's Eye View Worksheet on page 87 shows how to paint the greenery, fence, and flowers on the base.

GATHER THESE SUPPLIES

Painting Surface:
Wooden birdhouse lamp,
  6" x 11½"
Wooden shade, 10" high,
  6" top diameter;
  10" bottom diameter

Paints, Stains, and Finishes:
Acrylic craft paints:
  Bayberry
  Burnt Umber
  Ivory White
  Licorice
  Light Periwinkle
  Lipstick Red
  Olive Green
  Purple Lilac
  Sterling Blue
  Sunflower
  Violet Pansy
Acrylic painting medium:
  extender
Waterbase varnish

Brushes:
Comb
Deerfoot brush
Flat brushes
Liner
Mop brush
Round brush
Sponge brush

Other Supplies:
Masking tape
Sandpaper: 220 grit

INSTRUCTIONS

Prepare and Base-coat:
1. Seal lamp and shade with waterbase varnish. Let dry. Sand smooth.

2. Paint shade, inside and out, with Ivory White.

3. Paint birdhouse walls and base with Light Periwinkle mixed with Ivory White.

4. Paint birdhouse roof with Ivory White.

5. Transfer Bird's Eye View Lamp Patterns on page 88.

6. Transfer outlines of nest to shade.

PAINT THE DESIGN

Greenery and Fence:
1. Measure 2" up from bottom edge of birdhouse. Mark a line around perimeter of birdhouse with a pencil. Stipple paint in this area using a deerfoot brush with Olive Green.

2. Stipple Bayberry across top of stippled section, blending colors. Add small leaves across top.

3. Using masking tape, mask off fence for painting. Horizontal rail is ¼" wide and 2" up from bottom edge of birdhouse. Pickets are ¼" wide.

4. Paint fence with Ivory White. For the gate, paint two pickets ¼" taller than rest of fence on front and add a diagonal picket. Let dry. Remove tape.

5. Paint vines, stems, and leaves with Olive Green and Bayberry.

Flowers Around Fence:
1. Paint iris blossoms with Violet Pansy and Purple Lilac.

2. Paint daisy blossoms with Ivory White. Add daisy centers with Sunflower and Lipstick Red.

3. Paint hollyhock blossoms with Lipstick Red mixed with Ivory White.

Sky Above Fence:
1. Paint clouds with a thin coat of Ivory White.

2. Paint breast of bird with Sunflower mixed with Lipstick Red. Paint remainder of bird with Burnt Umber.

3. Paint butterfly wings with Sunflower mixed with Lipstick Red. Outline with Licorice.

Lampshade Background:
1. Paint outer edge of background with a thin, light blue mix of Bayberry and Sterling Blue mixed with Ivory White.

2. Layer a mix of Olive Green, Sunflower, and Ivory White over background. Let dry.

3. Transfer pattern details.

4. Paint leaves and stems with a mix of Olive Green, Sunflower, and Ivory White.

5. Spatter scene with Olive Green.

Nest and Birds:
1. Base-coat nest with Sunflower and Burnt Umber. Shade lower edge of nest with Burnt Umber, blending colors into background.

2. Using a round brush, paint grass in nest with Sunflower mixed with Ivory White.

3. Paint breasts of birds with Sunflower mixed with Lipstick Red. Shade with Burnt Umber.

4. Paint heads, wings, and backs with Sterling Blue and Ivory White. Highlight with Ivory White.

5. Add beaks with Sunflower. Highlight with Ivory White.

6. Dot eyes with Licorice. Outline with Ivory White. Highlight pupils with Ivory White.

7. Outline beaks and some feathers with Licorice.

8. Add a few strands of grass, overlapping the birds.

Flowers on Lampshade:
1. Paint blossoms with a mix of Sterling Blue and Ivory White.

2. Lighten with Ivory White. Add centers with Sterling Blue and Licorice. Let dry.

FINISH

1. Paint strip around edge of lamp base with Ivory White. Let dry.

2. Apply waterbase varnish to shade and base of lamp.

Village Antiques Birdhouse

Pictured on page 89

Designed by
Chris Stokes

This painted stone cottage has a copper roof. The door, window, window box, and signs are separate pieces that are painted and glued on to add dimension. Dried flowers adorn the window box.

GATHER THESE SUPPLIES

Painting Surface:
Wooden birdhouse

Paints, Stains, and Finishes:
Acrylic craft paints:
    Barnyard Red
    Bayberry
    Burnt Umber
    Charcoal Gray
    Honeycomb
    Hunter Green
    Licorice
    Purple
    Sunflower
    Taffy
    Wicker White
Metallic acrylic craft paint:
    Pure Gold
Antiquing medium:
    Down Home Brown
Waterbase varnish

Brushes:
Fan brush
Flat brushes
Liner
Sponge brush

Other Supplies:
Thin copper sheeting for roof
Permanent black ink pen
Hot glue gun & glue sticks
Liver of sulfur
Sea sponge
Small brads
Small dried flowers

INSTRUCTIONS

Prepare and Stain:
1. Prepare wood. See Surface Preparation on page 7.

2. Mix Down Home Brown antiquing medium with water and stain entire house inside and out. Let dry.

3. Transfer Village Antiques Birdhouse Pattern on page 91.

PAINT THE DESIGN

Walls and Chimney:
1. Using a sea sponge, pounce in Burnt Umber, Honeycomb, and a touch of Taffy on house walls and chimney. Let dry.

2. Using a liner, wiggle mortar between stones with Charcoal Gray and Licorice.

3. Randomly highlight stones with floats of Taffy and Sunflower.

Base:
1. Paint with Hunter Green mixed with a touch of Sunflower. Let dry.

2. Pounce steps and path in same manner as walls and chimney, using same colors.

Continued on 90

Bird's Eye View Worksheet

1. Using a deerfoot brush or small sponge, stipple with Olive Green to base-coat the bushy area.

2. Stipple Bayberry across the top of the base-coated area and blend the two colors together. Paint small leaves across the top edge.

3. Using masking tape, mask off fence pickets. Paint pickets with Ivory White. Let dry. Remove tape.

4. Paint the dark leaves and stems with Olive Green and the light leaves with Bayberry. Paint the flowers a variety of colors from the palette.

Bird's Eye View Lamp Patterns

Lamp Shade

Enlarge pattern 110%

Base

Enlarge pattern 110%

Continued from page 86

Door and Window:
1. Paint door with Barnyard Red. Shade with Licorice. Highlight with Taffy.

2. Paint door window with Charcoal Gray. Paint window panes with Taffy.

3. Paint sign above door with Taffy. Trim sign and outline with Barnyard Red. Letter "Welcome" with black ink pen.

Front Window:
1. Base-coat with Charcoal Gray.

2. Paint frame with Barnyard Red. Outline with Taffy.

3. Float lamp chimney with Wicker White. Float lamp globe with Sunflower.

4. Paint rose on lamp with double loaded Wicker White and Barnyard Red. Paint leaves Hunter Green and Taffy. Using a liner, paint brass area of lamp with Pure Gold.

5. Float curtains with Wicker White. Paint edges of curtains with squiggles of Wicker White.

6. Paint window box with Barnyard Red.

Sign Above Window:
1. Paint with Sunflower. Shade with Burnt Umber.

2. Letter "Village Antiques" with black ink pen.

Irises Along Walls:
1. Using a fan brush, pull up leaves with inky Hunter Green and Licorice. Reload with Bayberry and pull up more leaves.

2. Pull up more leaves, using a liner and the same colors.

3. Pounce in flowers with doubled loaded Purple and Taffy and with Barnyard Red and Sunflower. Let dry.

FINISH

1. Hot-glue copper sheeting to roof. Use small brads to nail the copper sheeting in place.

2. Using a sponge brush with downward strokes, antique the copper with liver of sulfur.

3. Apply waterbase varnish to everything but the copper. Let dry.

4. Hot-glue all small wood pieces in place, using photo as a guide for placement.

5. Hot-glue small dried flowers in window box.

Birdie Mansion

Pictured on pages 92 and 93

Designed by
Alma Lynne

A seed packet design and a checked roof adorn this simple birdhouse. The pole is wrapped with a coordinating print fabric and finished with a bow. (Of course, you wouldn't use fabric on an outdoor birdhouse.)

GATHER THESE SUPPLIES

Painting Surface:
Wooden birdhouse on stand, 7½" x 7½" x 9"

Paints, Stains, and Finishes:
Acrylic craft paints:
  Buckskin Brown
  Burgundy
  Engine Red
  Green
  Huckleberry
  Hunter Green
  Licorice
  True Blue
  Wicker White
Acrylic painting medium:
  extender
Matte spray sealer

Brushes:
Angle shaders
Flat brush
Round brushes
Script liner
Sponge brush

Other Supplies:
Print fabric: ½ yd.
Hot glue gun & glue sticks
Permanent black ink pen
Spanish moss

INSTRUCTIONS

Prepare and Base-coat:
1. Prepare wood. See Surface Preparation on page 7.

2. Paint birdhouse with Wicker White. Let dry.

3. Using a flat brush, paint checkerboard squares on roof with True Blue.

4. Paint around edges of roof with True Blue.

Village Antiques Birdhouse Pattern

Enlarge pattern 200%

Birdie Mansion
Instructions begin on page 90

Continued from page 90

5. Paint front, back, perch and edge of base of birdhouse with Engine Red.

6. Transfer Birdie Mansion Pattern on page 95 to sides of birdhouse.

PAINT THE DESIGN

Seed Packet:
1. Wash seed packet with Buckskin Brown.

2. Paint flower on seed packet with Engine Red. Paint leaves with Hunter Green.

3. Highlight leaves and flower on seed packet with Wicker White.

4. Paint "5 cents" with Licorice.

5. Letter "FLOWERS" with Engine Red.

6. Paint flower pot with Huckleberry. Highlight with Buckskin Brown.

Flowers in Pot:
1. Paint flowers with Engine Red. Shade with Burgundy. Highlight with strokes of Wicker White mixed with a small amount of Engine Red.

2. Paint leaves with Hunter Green. Highlight with Green. Let dry.

FINISH

1. Add details, outlines, and lettering with black ink pen. Let dry.

2. Spray with matte spray sealer. Let dry.

3. Glue moss in entrance hole.

4. Glue fabric around pole.

5. Cut or tear a piece of fabric to make a bow. Tie bow around pole below birdhouse.

Birdhouse Mailbox

Pictured on page 96

Designed by
Donna Dewberry

A trio of birdhouses adorns this charming mailbox. The design may be painted on one or both sides.

GATHER THESE SUPPLIES

Painting Surface:
White rural mailbox

Paints, Stains, and Finishes:
Acrylic craft paints:
    Burnt Umber
    Camel
    Green Forest
    Licorice
    Nutmeg
    Prussian Blue
    Raspberry Wine
    Wicker White
Matte spray sealer

Brushes:
Flat brush
Script liner

INSTRUCTIONS

Prepare and Base-coat:
1. Prepare surface. See Surface Preparation on page 7.

2. Transfer Birdhouse Mailbox Patterns on pages 98 and 99.

PAINT THE DESIGN

Birdhouses:
1. Load a flat brush with Camel. Base-coat all three birdhouses.

2. Load a flat brush with Camel and Nutmeg. Shade outer edges of left birdhouse while basecoat is still wet.

3. Load a flat brush with Raspberry Wine. Shade edges of right birdhouse, blending toward center.

4. Load a flat brush with inky Raspberry Wine. Lightly shade center birdhouse. Let dry.

Door, Pot, and Shingle Roof:
1. Load a flat brush with Raspberry Wine. Paint door of right birdhouse.

2. Paint pot with Raspberry Wine.

3. With chisel edge of brush, paint shingle roof of center birdhouse with Raspberry Wine.

Blue Roofs:
1. Load a flat brush with Prussian Blue. Paint roofs of left and right birdhouses. Let dry.

Tree Trunk and Battens:
1. Load a flat brush with Burnt Umber. Paint tree trunk and batten lines on left birdhouse, using chisel edge of brush. Let dry.

Continued on page 97

Continued from page 94

Entrance Holes:
1. Load flat brush with Licorice. Paint circles to form entrance holes. Let dry.

Black Accents:
1. Load script liner with inky Licorice. Using tip of brush, paint perches, accents on battens of left birdhouse, horizontal accents on center birdhouse, and "Welcome" on right birdhouse.

Blueberry Vines and Blueberries:
1. Double-load flat brush with Green Forest and Wicker White. Paint vines with chisel edge of brush. Paint leaves. See Leaves Worksheet on page 51.

2. Load handle end of flat brush with Prussian Blue. Dot on berries. Let dry.

Vines with Red Berries:
1. Load script liner with Green Forest. Using chisel edge, paint vines.

2. Load handle end of script liner with Raspberry Wine. Dot on berries.

Moss and Tree:
1. Load a flat brush with Wicker White, Green Forest, and Burnt Umber. Stipple moss along bottom edge of mailbox, across top of left birdhouse, and up left side of right birdhouse.

2. Load flat brush with Wicker White, Burnt Umber, and Green Forest. Stipple tree top. Use more Green Forest for tree top than was used for moss, especially at edges of tree top.

3. Load script liner with inky Green Forest. Paint vines on tree top.

Highlights:
1. Load script liner with Wicker White. Paint highlights on entrance holes and perches. Let dry.

FINISH

1. Spray with two coats of matte spray sealer.

Quilted Landscape Birdhouse

Pictured on page 100

Designed by
Julie Watkins Schreiner

Snowcapped mountains and pine trees grace the sides of this colorful painted and stenciled birdhouse. Details are added with a fine-point permanent black ink pen.

GATHER THESE SUPPLIES

Painting Surface:
Wooden birdhouse on stand, 7½" x 7½" x 9"

Paints, Stains, and Finishes:
Acrylic craft paints:
Apple Spice
Baby Blue
Bayberry
Buttercup
Clover
Heather
Honeycomb
Purple Passion
Southern Pine
Thunder Blue
Violet Pansy
Wicker White
Yellow Ochre
Matte spray sealer

Brushes:
Round brushes
Sponge brush
Stencil brush

Other Supplies:
Permanent black ink pen
Stencils: stripes, stars & moon

INSTRUCTIONS

Prepare and Base-coat:
1. Prepare wood. See Surface Preparation on page 7.

2. Paint roof of house with Thunder Blue. Let dry.

3. Stencil lines on roof with Baby Blue. Stencil lines in one direction, then in the other direction to create a plaid look.

4. Transfer Quilted Landscape Birdhouse Patterns on pages 102 and 103 to walls and roof of house.

PAINT THE DESIGN

Walls:
1. Paint design with colors indicated on pattern. Let dry.

2. Stencil small stars on birdhouse with Baby Blue.

3. Stencil horizontal bars on Violet Pansy mountains with Heather.

Continued on page 101

Birdhouse Mailbox Patterns

Pattern is actual size

Quilted Landscape Birdhouse
Instructions begin on page 97

Continued from page 97

4. Stencil vertical lines on Clover trees with Yellow Ochre.

Roof:
1. Paint moon and stars on roof using stencils.

Perch, Entrance, and Base:
1. Paint perch with Buttercup.

2. Paint inside of entrance hole with Thunder Blue.

3. Paint base of house with Apple Spice.

Stand and Pole:
1. Paint base of stand with Clover. Let dry.

2. Use stencil to make plaid on base with Yellow Ochre, using same method as on roof.

3. Stencil large stars around sides of base of stand with Apple Spice.

4. Paint pole with Honeycomb. Let dry.

5. Stencil stars around pole with Thunder Blue. Let dry.

FINISH

1. Using a black ink pen, draw stitch lines on sections of pattern to create an appliqué look.

2. Spray with matte spray sealer.

Ivy Heart Wreath Tee

Pictured on page 104

Designed by
Donna Dewberry

Here are birdhouses to wear — framed with a heart-shaped vine wreath and twining ivy. Techniques are highlighted on the Birdhouses and Wildflowers Worksheet on page 109.

GATHER THESE SUPPLIES

Painting Surface:
Natural tee shirt

Paints, Stains, and Finishes:
Acrylic craft paints:
    Berry Wine
    Country Twill
    Dark Brown
    Green Forest
    Leaf Green
    Licorice
    Midnight
    Wicker White
Acrylic painting medium:
    textile

Brushes:
Flat brush
Script liner

Other Supplies:
Disappearing pen
Fine-point permanent marker
Masking tape
Shirtboard
Tulle (nylon netting)

Note: A shirtboard can be purchased or made. To make a shirtboard, cut a piece of cardboard large enough to fit inside the garment. Cover cardboard with plastic wrap.

INSTRUCTIONS

Prepare Tee Shirt:
1. Wash and dry the garment according to manufacturer's directions to remove sizing and excess dye and guard against shrinkage after painting. Do not use fabric softener. Iron the garment.

2. Place a piece of tulle over the Ivy Heart Wreath Tee Pattern on page 106 and trace pattern on the tulle with a fine-point permanent marker. Position the tulle on the tee shirt and transfer the pattern by redrawing over the lines with a disappearing pen.

3. Place a cardboard shirtboard inside tee shirt. Use masking tape to fasten excess fabric to back of shirtboard, out of the way. The painting surface should be taut and flat, but not stretched out of shape.

Prepare Paint:
1. On paint palette, mix one part textile medium with two parts of each acrylic paint color.

2. Test fabric by applying a little paint in an inconspicuous part of the garment, such as a seam allowance or hem.

PAINT THE DESIGN

1. Paint vines with a multi-loaded flat brush of Dark Brown, Country Twill, and Wicker White. See Birdhouses and Wildflowers Worksheet on page 109.

Continued on page 105

Quilted Landscape Birdhouse Patterns

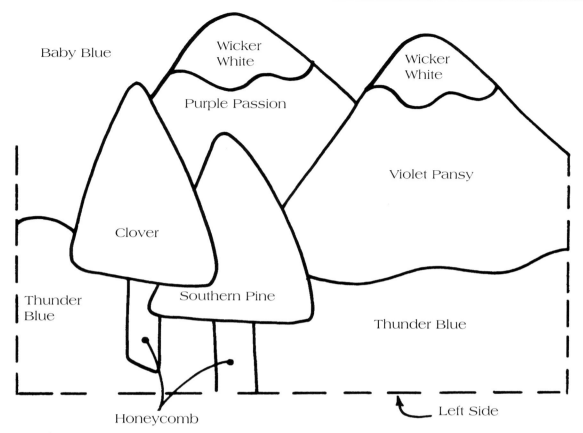

Baby Blue

Wicker White

Purple Passion

Wicker White

Violet Pansy

Clover

Thunder Blue

Southern Pine

Thunder Blue

Honeycomb

Left Side

Patterns are actual size

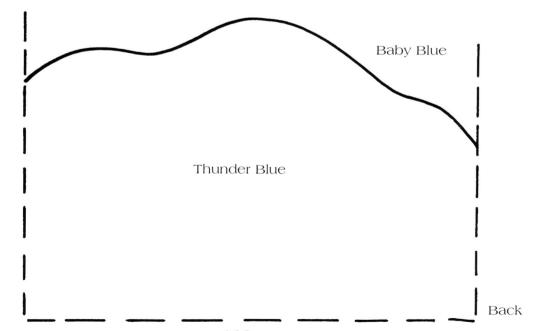

Baby Blue

Thunder Blue

Back

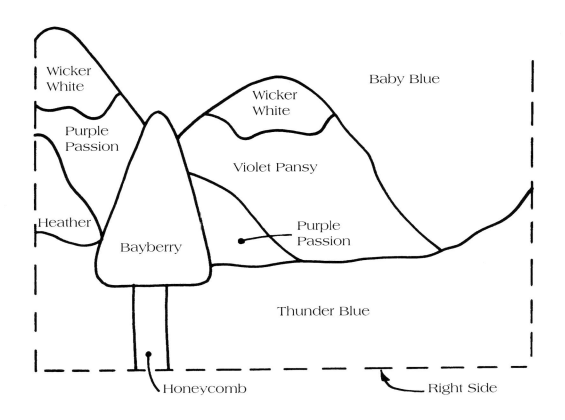

Wicker White

Purple Passion

Heather

Bayberry

Wicker White

Violet Pansy

Baby Blue

Purple Passion

Thunder Blue

Honeycomb

Right Side

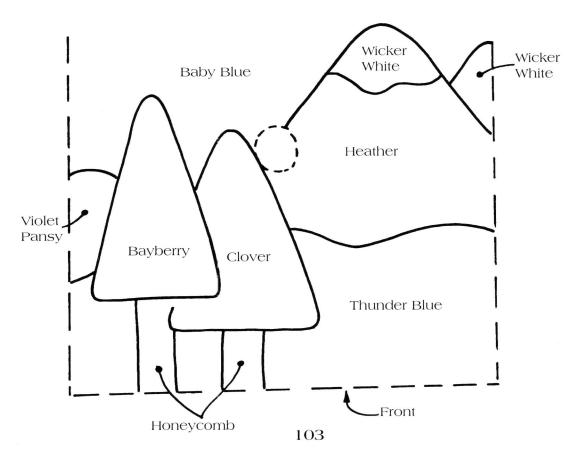

Baby Blue

Wicker White

Wicker White

Heather

Violet Pansy

Bayberry

Clover

Thunder Blue

Honeycomb

Front

103

Birdhouses & Wildflowers Tee
Instructions begin on page 105

Ivy Heart Wreath Tee
Instructions begin on page 101

Continued from page 101

2. Paint walls of birdhouse with multi-loaded Country Twill and White. Let dry.

3. Using a script liner, paint vertical lines on walls of birdhouse with Dark Brown.

4. Using a flat brush, paint birdhouse opening with Licorice. Highlight with Wicker White. Using chisel edge of brush, paint perch.

5. Using chisel edge of brush, paint roof with Midnight.

6. Paint leaves multi-loaded with Green Forest and Leaf Green. See Birdhouses and Wildflowers Worksheet on page 109.

7. Using a script liner, paint tendrils with Green Forest.

8. Paint heart on birdhouse with Berry Wine.

9. Paint bow with Berry Wine.

FINISH

1. Let paint dry for at least 24 hours.

2. Heat-set by placing a pressing cloth over painted design. Iron for 30 seconds over pressing cloth with iron on highest appropriate setting for fabric.

Birdhouses & Wildflowers Tee

Pictured on page 104

Designed by
Donna Dewberry

Birdhouses and wildflowers grace this garden scene on a tee shirt. See the Birdhouses & Wildflowers Worksheet on page 109 to demonstrate painting techniques for birdhouses and wildflowers.

GATHER THESE SUPPLIES

Painting Surface:
White tee shirt

Paints, Stains, and Finishes:
Acrylic craft paints:
   Berry Wine
   Country Twill
   Dark Brown
   Fuchsia
   Green Forest
   Leaf Green
   Midnight
   School Bus Yellow
   Violet Pansy
   Wicker White
Acrylic painting medium:
   textile

Brushes:
Flat brush
Script liner

Additional Supplies:
Fine-point permanent marker
Disappearing pen
Shirtboard
Tulle (nylon netting)

Note: A shirtboard can be purchased or made. To make a shirtboard, cut a piece of cardboard large enough to fit inside the garment. Cover cardboard with plastic wrap.

INSTRUCTIONS

Prepare Tee Shirt:
1. Wash and dry the garment according to manufacturer's directions to remove sizing and excess dye and guard against shrinkage after painting. Do not use fabric softener. Iron the garment.

2. Place a piece of tulle over the Birdhouses & Wildflowers Tee Pattern on page 108 and trace pattern on the tulle with a fine-point permanent marker. Position the tulle on the tee shirt and transfer the pattern by redrawing over the lines with a disappearing pen.

3. Place a cardboard shirtboard inside tee shirt. Use masking tape to fasten excess fabric to back of shirtboard, out of the way. The painting surface should be taut and flat, but not stretched out of shape.

Prepare Paint:
1. On paint palette, mix one part textile medium with two parts of each acrylic paint color.

2. Test fabric by applying a little paint in an inconspicuous part of the garment, such as a seam allowance or hem.
Continued on page 107

Ivy Heart Wreath Tee Pattern

Pattern is actual size

Continued from page 105

PAINT THE DESIGN

1. Double-load a flat brush with Country Twill and Wicker White. Paint birdhouses and poles. See Birdhouses & Wildflowers Worksheet on page 109.

2. Double-load a flat brush with Berry Wine and Wicker White. Paint roof shingles.

3. Paint entrance holes and perches with Dark Brown. Highlight with Wicker White.

4. Using a flat brush, paint stippled greenery at base of shirt and along poles and atop birdhouses with Green Forest or Leaf Green and Wicker White. You can also add some School Bus Yellow to some of the stippling.

5. Add vines with Leaf Green.

6. Paint leaves, plant foliage, and grass with Wicker White and Green Forest. Paint grass with chisel edge of brush, stroking up from the bottom.

7. Paint various flowers.

8. Using chisel edge of brush, paint tiny "V" shapes in sky with Midnight to look like birds flying.

FINISH

1. Let paint dry for at least 24 hours.

2. Heat-set by placing a pressing cloth over painted design. Iron for 30 seconds over pressing cloth with iron or highest appropriate setting for fabric.

Starburst Summer Birdhouse

Pictured on page 110

Designed by
Chris Stokes

This birdhouse, with its simple stenciled design, is a perfect centerpiece for a summer cookout.

GATHER THESE SUPPLIES

Painting Surface:
Wooden birdhouse planter, 5¾" x 6¾" x 7½"

Paints, Stains, and Finishes:
Acrylic craft paints:
  Huckleberry
  Navy Blue
  Taffy
Antiquing medium:
  Down Home Brown
Matte spray sealer

Brushes:
Stencil brush
Sponge brush

Other Supplies:
Assorted decorative foliage
Floral foam
Masking tape: ¾" wide
Sandpaper
Spanish moss
Stars & bars stencil
White craft glue
Wire
Wooden stars: ¾" thick, assorted sizes from 2" to 4" (9)

INSTRUCTIONS

Prepare and Stain:
1. Prepare wood. See Surface Preparation on page 7.

2. Mix Down Home Brown antiquing medium with water and stain wood. Let dry.

Paint:
1. Paint entire front and back of house with Taffy.

2. Paint sides and roof with Navy Blue. Let dry.

3. Using masking tape, mask off stripes on front and back of house.

4. Using a stencil brush, dab Huckleberry onto stripes. Wipe excess paint away with a paper towel. Let dry. Remove tape.

5. Stencil small stars from pre-cut stencil on white stripes with Navy Blue. See Starburst Summer Birdhouse House Pattern on page 111.

6. Stencil various sizes of stars on sides and roof of house with Taffy. See Starburst Summer Birdhouse Roof Pattern on page 112. Let dry.

7. Paint wooden stars with Navy Blue, Taffy, and Huckleberry. Let dry.

FINISH

1. Sand edges of birdhouse and wooden stars.

2. Spray house and stars with matte spray sealer.
Continued on page 112

Birdhouses & Wildflowers Tee Pattern

Pattern is actual size

Birdhouses & Wildflowers Worksheet

Birdhouse Body
Stroke each side with flat brush multi-loaded with Country Twill and Wicker White. Turn Country Twill side toward outside.

Fill in center.

Roof
Multi-load flat brush with Wicker White and Midnight and make small 'U' strokes. Turn Midnight side toward bottom.

Continue "U" strokes for roof in staggered rows. Work upward. Make strokes smaller while working toward top. Reverse colors when painting roof tile design on Wildflower Birdhouse. (Turn Wicker White side toward bottom.)

Inside hole shadowing

Bottom
Midnight; using script liner.

Grass & Vines
Multi-load flat brush with Wicker White and Green Forest. Make short upward strokes. Use light, brisk strokes on chisel edge.

Hole & Perch
Paint with Dark Brown using script liner. Highlight with Wicker White.

Bow
Berry Wine using script liner.

Push   Turn

Lift

Chisel edge

Leaves
Add one-stroke leaves to vine. Multi-load Wicker White and Green Forest using a flat brush.

Greenery, Grass, Bushes
Stipple grass with a flat brush loaded with either Green Forest or Leaf Green and Wicker White. Flowers can be stippled in same manner with flower color and Wicker White.

Plant
Paint with chisel edge. Multi-load Wicker White and Green Forest using a flat brush.

Use tip of flat brush

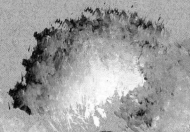

Multi-load Dioxazine Purple and Wicker White. Using chisel edge, make short downward strokes.

Poles
Multi-load a flat with Wicker White and Country Twill. Pull from top downward.

Flowers
Multi-load a flat brush with School Bus Yellow and Wicker White. Dab flowers.

Multi-load brush with Midnight and Wicker White. Make "C" stroke for each petal; turn Midnight side toward outside. Make 5 or 6 petals.

Multi-load a flat brush with Berry Wine and Wicker White; small "C" stroke to form petal.

Dot with handle end of brush.

Starburst Summer Birdhouse
House Pattern

Enlarge pattern 105%

Starburst Summer Birdhouse Roof Pattern

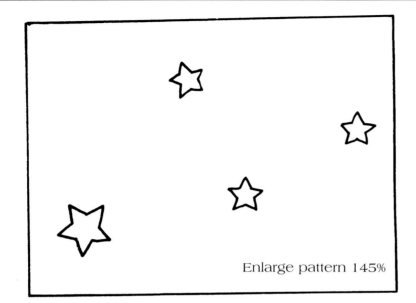

Enlarge pattern 145%

Continued from page 107

3. Place floral foam in birdhouse. Arrange greenery.

4. Cut wire to various lengths. Glue wooden stars to lengths of wire. Insert wire in foam.

5. Place Spanish moss in birdhouse entrance hole.

Grapes & Moss Hanging Birdhouse

Pictured on page 113

Designed by
Donna Dewberry

Grapes and moss adorn this birdhouse. Painting techniques for grapes, leaves, and vines are illustrated on the Grapes & Moss Worksheet on page 114.

GATHER THESE SUPPLIES

Painting Surface:
Wooden birdhouse, 13" tall

Paints, Stains, and Finishes:
Acrylic craft paints:
   Dioxazine Purple
   Green Forest
   Maple Syrup
   Olive Green
   Sunflower
   Wicker White
White primer
Matte spray sealer

Brushes:
Flat brushes
Script liner

Other Supplies:
Metal eye screw
Sandpaper: 220 grit
Tack cloth

INSTRUCTIONS

Prepare and Base-coat:
1. Prepare wood. See Surface Preparation on page 7.

2. Apply white primer according to manufacturer's directions. Let dry.

3. Paint with two coats of Wicker White. Let dry.

4. Load a flat brush with Green Forest, Olive Green, and Maple Syrup. Lightly pounce brush on roof, around base, around opening, and on other areas of birdhouse. Let dry.

5. Trace and transfer Grapes & Moss Hanging Birdhouse Pattern on page 115.

PAINT THE DESIGN

1. Load brush with Maple Syrup mixed with Wicker White. Paint vines. See Grapes & Moss Worksheet on page 114.

2. Double-load a flat brush with Sunflower mixed with Green Forest. Paint leaves.

3. Using a script liner, paint curlicues with inky Maple Syrup. Paint additional curlicues with inky Green Forest.

4. Paint grapes. Let dry.

FINISH

1. Spray with matte spray sealer.

Grapes & Moss Worksheet

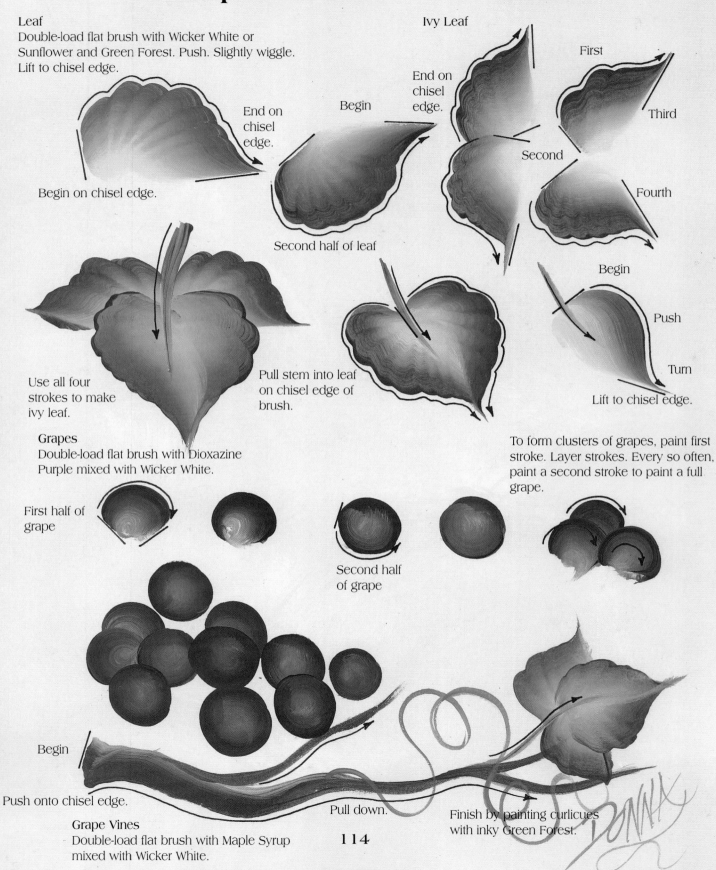

Leaf
Double-load flat brush with Wicker White or Sunflower and Green Forest. Push. Slightly wiggle. Lift to chisel edge.

Begin on chisel edge.

End on chisel edge.

Begin

Second half of leaf

Ivy Leaf

End on chisel edge.

First

Second

Third

Fourth

Begin

Push

Turn

Lift to chisel edge.

Use all four strokes to make ivy leaf.

Pull stem into leaf on chisel edge of brush.

Grapes
Double-load flat brush with Dioxazine Purple mixed with Wicker White.

To form clusters of grapes, paint first stroke. Layer strokes. Every so often, paint a second stroke to paint a full grape.

First half of grape

Second half of grape

Begin

Push onto chisel edge.

Pull down.

Finish by painting curlicues with inky Green Forest.

Grape Vines
Double-load flat brush with Maple Syrup mixed with Wicker White.

114

Grapes & Moss Hanging Birdhouse Pattern

Pattern is actual size

Tudor Birdhouse

Pictured on page 116

Designed by
Kathi Malarchuk

This charming cottage has faux stucco walls and trailing vines with heart-shaped leaves. Washes of color and the tiny shutters add to its rustic appeal.

GATHER THESE SUPPLIES

Painting Surface:
Wooden birdhouse,
7½" x 4" x 9¼"

Paints, Stains, and Finishes:
Acrylic craft paints:
Aspen Green
Burnt Sienna
Clover
Licorice
Light Gray
Medium Gray
Napthol Crimson
Wicker White
Matte spray sealer

Brushes:
Flat brush
Liner
Round brush
Sponge brush

Other Supplies:
Masking tape: ¾"
Paper towels

INSTRUCTIONS

Prepare:
1. Prepare wood. See Surface Preparation on page 7.

2. Paint entire house with Wicker White.

3. Paint inside edge of openings with Licorice. Let dry.

4. Mask off door, chimney, and shutters with tape. Dilute 1 teaspoon of Clover with an equal amount of water to create a wash. Wash body of house. While paint is still wet, pounce a crumbled paper towel over paint to create a texture. Let dry. Remove tape.

5. Transfer Tudor Birdhouse Stone Pattern on page 118 to door and chimney of house.

6. Transfer Tudor Birdhouse Vine Pattern on page 118 to house. Repeat vine randomly.

PAINT THE DESIGN

1. Paint roof with Light Gray.

2. Wash over roof with Medium Gray. Let dry.

3. Mask off stripes on roof with tape. Paint stripes on roof and center beam on roof with Medium Gray. Remove tape. Let dry.

4. Paint steps with Burnt Sienna. Shade with Licorice. Highlight with Wicker White. Let dry.

5. Paint remainder of base with Clover.

6. Double-load a flat brush with Light Gray and Medium Gray. Paint stones. Let dry.

7. Paint heart-shaped leaves on vines, use a round brush with Aspen Green, painting two teardrop strokes joined in the center. Highlight leaves with Wicker White.

8. Using a liner brush, outline leaves with Licorice.

9. Dip handle end of brush in Napthol Crimson. Dot on vines to create flowers.

10. Using a liner brush, paint stems, tendrils, and grass at base with Aspen Green.

11. Paint hearts on door and shutters with Napthol Crimson. Let dry.

FINISH

1. Spray with matte spray sealer.

Wren's House Painting

Pictured on page 119

Designed by
Dolores Lennon

At home almost anywhere, our little friend has especially nice lodgings in our painting. This painting is done with an ink and wash technique.

GATHER THESE SUPPLIES

Painting Surface:
Watercolor paper, 11" x 12"

Paints, Stains, and Finishes:
Acrylic craft paints:
Bluebonnet
Burnt Sienna
Burnt Umber
Buttercup

Tudor Birdhouse Patterns

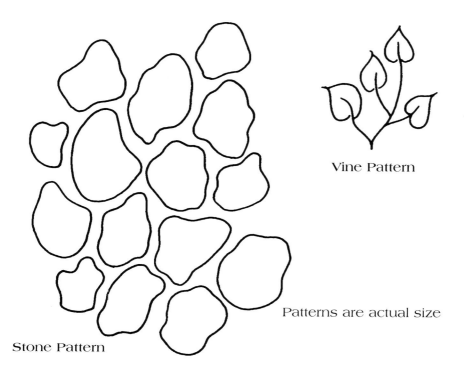

Vine Pattern

Patterns are actual size

Stone Pattern

Christmas Red
English Mustard
Fresh Foliage
Nutmeg
Raspberry Wine
Southern Pine
Thicket
Wrought Iron

Brushes:
Round brush

Other Supplies:
Mat, 11" x 12"
Permanent black ink pen
Cardboard, 12" x 14"
Masking tape

INSTRUCTIONS

1. Transfer Wren's House Painting Pattern on page 120 to paper.

2. Using masking tape, tape paper to cardboard.

3. Carefully ink the design. Let dry.

PAINT THE DESIGN

Bird's Feet and Beak:
1. Dampen area. Fill in areas with a wash of Burnt Sienna mixed with Christmas Red.

2. Make a shadow at the base of beak and on feet under body with a Nutmeg wash.

Body:
1. Wet entire body except eye, chin, and breast. Fill in this area with a wash of Nutmeg. Apply a very thin wash of Nutmeg to remaining body.

2. Touch down thinned Burnt Sienna on body (starting on the tail) and wing feathers. Use the very tip of the round brush. Pick up more Burnt Sienna on tip of brush and repeat while areas are still damp (touch paper to be certain). If not damp, re-dampen with clean water first.

3. Add touches of a Raspberry Wine wash to bird's back and top of head.

Birdhouse:
1. Wet house. Apply a wash of Bluebonnet.

2. Color shadow areas on roof and under roof and nails with a wash of Burnt Sienna, then with a wash of Burnt Umber while house is still damp. (If not damp, re-dampen with clean water.)

Daisies:
1. Do one daisy petal at a time. Dampen a petal. Apply a wash of Wrought Iron to base of petal (end nearest center). Make this very faint. Tint each petal at base and along one edge and tip with thinned Raspberry Wine.

2. Apply a wash of English Mustard to centers. Then apply a Buttercup wash to upper half of centers.

Leaves:
1. Make washes of Fresh Foliage, Thicket, and Southern Pine.

Continued on page 122

Wren's House Painting
Instructions begin on page 117

Wren's House Painting Pattern

Pattern is actual size

Haunted Birdhouse
Instructions begin on page 123

Pumpkin Birdhouse
Instructions begin on page 122

Continued from page 118

2. Dampen leaves. Fill in leaves, coloring book style, with washes of Fresh Foliage or Thicket. Apply Southern Pine to shade areas at base of leaf.

3. Apply accent color by first dampening a small area or edge with clean water, then washing with Bluebonnet or Raspberry Wine.

Shadows Under House:
1. Dampen area and wash with Bluebonnet.

2. Wash Wrought Iron directly under house for deepest shading. Let dry thoroughly.

FINISH

1. Re-ink details on bird and house. Let dry.

2. Mat and frame painting.

Pumpkin Birdhouse

Pictured on page 121

Designed by
Kathi Malarchuk

Decorate a birdhouse especially for the fall season. Your little birdie tenants would love to see their abode redecorated for the season.

GATHER THESE SUPPLIES

Surface:
Round top wooden
   birdhouse, 6¾" x 5" x 8"

Paints, Stains, and Finishes:
Acrylic craft paints:
   Autumn Leaves
   Cappuccino
   Burnt Umber
   Country Twill
   Nutmeg
   Olive Green
   Parchment
   Wicker White
Matte spray sealer

Brushes:
Flat brushes
Liner

Other Supplies:
Masking tape
Pencil with clean erasure tip
Sandpaper

INSTRUCTIONS

Prepare and Base-coat:
1. Prepare wood. See Surface Preparation on page 7.

2. Using masking tape, protect roof and base while base-coating house with two coats of Parchment. Sand between coats.

3. Using masking tape, mark off squares for patches around sides of house.

PAINT THE DESIGN

Patches:
1. Paint squares Country Twill and Cappuccino and leave some squares Parchment. Let dry. Remove tape.

Wren's House Painting Color Washes

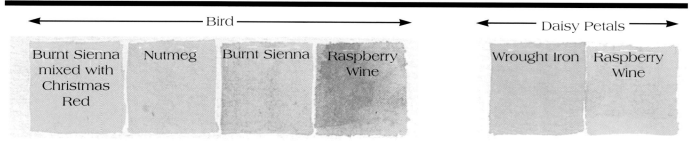

Bird — Burnt Sienna mixed with Christmas Red | Nutmeg | Burnt Sienna | Raspberry Wine

Daisy Petals — Wrought Iron | Raspberry Wine

2. Dip erasure tip of pencil into Burnt Umber and then dab onto Country Twill patches to form polka dots.

Plaid:

1. Thin Olive Green by mixing with water to create a wash. Load flat brush with wash to paint parallel lines, horizontal and vertical, ½" apart on Parchment patches. Load liner with Country Twill to paint one parallel line on each side of both horizontal and vertical stripes.

Pumpkins:

1. Transfer Pumpkin Birdhouse Pattern on page 125 to birdhouse, repeating pattern around sides of house.

2. Load a flat brush with Autumn Leaves to paint pumpkin sections. Sideload with Nutmeg to shade pumpkins. Sideload with Wicker White to highlight.

Pumpkin Greenery:

1. Double-load with Nutmeg and Burnt Umber for stems.

2. Paint leaves with Olive Green. Highlight with Wicker White.

3. Using a liner, paint tendrils with Olive Green.

FINISH

1. Paint stitches for patches with Burnt Umber.

2. Paint base and roof of house with a wash of Nutmeg. Let dry.

3. Spray with matte spray sealer.

Haunted Birdhouse

Pictured on page 121

Designed by
Julie Watkins Schreiner

This would make a charming decorative piece for your Halloween table as only scary birds can live here.

GATHER THESE SUPPLIES

Painting Surface:
Wooden birdhouse,
   5" x 4½" x 7"

Paints, Stains, and Finishes:
Acrylic craft paints:
   Dove Gray
   Licorice
   Pure Orange
   Purple Passion
   Raw Sienna
   Shamrock
   Wicker White
   Yellow Light
Matte spray sealer

Brushes:
Flat brush
Round brush

Other Supplies:
Small pieces of cut straw
Tacky glue

INSTRUCTIONS

Prepare and Base-coat:
1. Prepare wood. See Surface Preparation on page 7.

2. Paint body of house with Wicker White.

3. Paint roof with Licorice.

4. Paint underside of roof with Purple Passion.

5. Paint base of house and inside opening with Shamrock.

PAINT THE DESIGN

1. Using a flat brush, paint horizontal lines with Raw Sienna to look like siding.

2. Load a flat brush with Dove Gray to paint ½" long shingles on roof. Make shingles imperfect for an aged appearance.

3. Transfer Haunted Birdhouse Pattern on page 124 to house, referring to the photo on page 121 for placement.

4. Paint ghost, door, and window frames with Wicker White.

5. Paint door with Purple Passion.

6. Paint steps with Dove Gray.

7. Paint pumpkin with Pure Orange.

8. Paint window shutters with Yellow Light.

9. Paint hole in door, spiders, face on pumpkin, face on ghost, lines on steps, details on window shutters, and inside windows with Licorice.

10. Paint door knob and spider eyes with Yellow Light.

FINISH

1. Glue pieces of straw around base of house.

2. Spray with matte spray sealer.

Haunted Birdhouse Patterns

Spider

Window & shutters

Ghost top & bottom

Pumpkin, door & steps

Patterns are actual size

Pumpkin Birdhouse Pattern

Enlarge pattern 130%

Metric Equivalency Chart

MM-Millimetres   CM-Centimetres

INCHES TO MILLIMETRES AND CENTIMETRES

INCHES	MM	CM	INCHES	CM	INCHES	CM
⅛	3	0.3	9	22.9	30	76.2
¼	6	0.6	10	25.4	31	78.7
⅜	13	1.3	12	30.5	33	83.8
½	16	1.6	13	33.0	34	86.4
⅝	19	1.9	14	35.6	35	88.9
¾	22	2.2	15	38.1	36	91.4
⅞	25	2.5	16	40.6	37	94.0
1	32	3.2	17	43.2	38	96.5
1¼	38	3.8	18	45.7	39	99.1
1½	44	4.4	19	48.3	40	101.6
2	51	5.1	20	50.8	41	104.1
2½	64	6.4	21	53.3	42	106.7
3	76	7.6	22	55.9	43	109.2
3½	89	8.9	23	58.4	44	111.8
4	102	10.2	24	61.0	45	114.3
4½	114	11.4	25	63.5	46	116.8
5	127	12.7	26	66.0	47	119.4
6	152	15.2	27	68.6	48	121.9
7	178	17.8	28	71.1	49	124.5
8	203	20.3	29	73.7	50	127.0

Product Names and Sources

Plaid Enterprises, Inc., Norcross, GA produces several types of paint used for decorative painting. Following are the product names and numbers.

FolkArt® Acrylic Colors:

401 True Blue
402 Light Blue
403 Navy Blue
404 Periwinkle
405 Teal
406 Hunter Green
407 Kelly Green
408 Green
410 Lavendar
411 Purple
412 Magenta
413 Pink
414 Cardinal Red
415 Maroon
416 Dark Brown
417 Teddy Bear Brown
418 Buckskin Brown
419 Teddy Bear Tan
420 Linen
421 Portrait Light
422 Portrait

424 Light Gray
425 Medium Gray
426 Dark Gray
427 Ivory White
428 Rose White
429 Winter White
430 Spring White
431 French Vanilla
432 Sunflower
433 Terra Cotta
434 Berry Wine
435 Napthol Crimson
436 Engine Red
437 Lipstick
438 Ballet Pink
439 Purple Lilac
440 Violet Pansy
441 Sterling Blue
442 Baby Blue
443 Night Sky
444 Patina
445 Mint Green
447 Leaf Green
448 Green Forest
449 Olive Green
450 Parchment
451 Cappuccino
452 Raw Sienna
463 Dioxide Purple
464 Ceroulean Blue

471 Green Umber
476 Asphaltum
477 Payne's Gray
479 Pure Black
480 Titanium White
481 Aqua
484 Brilliant Ultramarine
485 Raw Umber
486 Prussian Blue
601 Clay Bisque
602 Country Twill
607 Settlers Blue
608 Heartland Blue
609 Thunder Blue
611 Barnyard Red
612 Holiday Red
613 Charcoal Gray
614 Buttercream
615 Georgia Peach
617 Peach Perfection
619 Poetry Green
620 Victorian Rose
624 Potpourri Rose

625 Lavendar Sachet
627 Tangerine
628 Pure Orange
629 Red Light
630 Poppy Red
632 Rise Pink
633 Baby Pink
634 Hot Pink
635 Fuchsia
636 Red Violet
637 Orchid
638 Purple Passion
639 French Blue
640 Light Periwinkle
641 Brilliant Blue
642 Blue Ink
643 Azure Blue
644 Grass Green
645 Basil Green
646 Aspen Green
647 Emerald Isle
649 Warm White
679 Turner's Yellow
686 Burnt Carmine
689 Pure Magenta
701 Icy White
702 Gray Mist
704 Milkshake

705 Almond Parfait
708 Dove Gray
711 Bluebonnet
713 Coastal Blue
715 Amish Blue
719 Blue Ribbon
720 Cobalt Blue
721 Denim Blue
723 Mystic Green
724 Evergreen
725 Tartan Green
726 Green Meadow
730 Southern Pine
733 Teal Green
735 Lemon Custard
736 School Bus Yellow
737 Buttercrunch
738 Peach Cobbler
741 Glazed Carrots
745 Huckleberry
747 Salmon
751 Strawberry Parfait
752 Berries 'n Cream
753 Rose Chiffon
754 Rose Garden

Product Names and Sources

758 Alizarin Crimson
759 Whipped Berry
761 Plum Chiffon
765 Porcelin Blue
767 Spring Rose
901 Wicker White
902 Taffy
903 Tapioca
904 Lemonade
905 Buttercup
906 Summer Sky
908 Indigo
909 Bluebell
910 Slate Blue
912 Promenade Coral
913 Cinnamon
914 Light Red Oxide
917 Yellow Ochre
918 Yellow Light
920 Autumn Leaves
922 Bayberry
923 Clover
924 Thicket
925 Wrought Iron
926 Shamrock
927 Oil Ivy
929 Cotton Candy

930 Primrose
932 Calico Red
933 Heather
934 Plum Pudding
935 Raspberry Wine
936 Barn Wood
937 Dapple Gray
938 Licorice
939 Butter Pecan
940 Coffee Bean
941 Acorn Brown
942 Honeycomb
943 Burnt Sienna
944 Nutmeg
945 Maple Syrup
949 Skintone
951 Apple Spice
953 Camel
954 Fresh Foliage
955 Sweetheart Pink
957 Burgundy
958 Christmas Red
959 English Mustard
961 Turquoise
962 Wintergreen
964 Midnight
966 Raspberry Sherbet

FolkArt® Metallic Colors:
651 Blue Topaz
652 Rose Shimmer
653 Emerald Green
654 Amethyst
655 Aquamarine
656 Blue Sapphire
657 Regal Red
658 Antique Gold
659 Pearl White
660 Pure Gold
661 Sequin Black
662 Silver Sterling
663 Solid Bronze
664 Copper
665 Garnet Red
666 Antique Copper
667 Gunmetal Gray
668 Plum
669 Periwinkle
670 Blue Pearl
671 Peridot
672 Mint Pearl
673 Rose Pearl
674 Peach Pearl
675 Champagne
676 Inca Gold

Apple Barrel® Gloss Enamel Colors:
20621 White
20622 Eggshell
20623 Antique White
20624 Dolphin Gray
20625 Deep Purple
20627 Purple Velvet
20629 Raspberry
20631 Pink Blush
20632 Holiday Rose
20633 Cranberry Red
20634 Rose Wine
20636 Real Red
20637 Hot Rod Red
20639 Tangerine
20643 Bermuda Beach
20645 Real Yellow
20646 Dandelion Yellow
20647 Crown Gold
20648 Mossy Green
20649 Forest Green

20651 Real Green
20652 Spring Green
20653 Arbor Green
20656 Lanier Blue
20657 Pinwheel Blue
20660 Real Blue
20661 Good-night Blue
20662 Black
20663 Beach-comber Beige
20665 Mocha
20666 Coffee Bean

Wooden Birdhouses are available from the following manufactuers:

Walnut Hollow
1409 State Road #23
Dodgeville, WI 53533

Provo Craft
285 E. 900 S.
Provo, UT 84606

Craft Cottage
223 Main Street
Dallas, GA 30132

Index